Within a Child's Heart

KAREN,

GREAT WISDOM COMES

FROM GREAT LESSONS

OF THE HEART!

06/11/02.

the real-life journey children face when their parents divorce

Within a Child's Heart:

Craig Henry Leibel

Inspire Media Inc.

Canadian Cataloguing in Publication Data
Leibel, Craig, 1973-
   Within a child's heart

   ISBN 0-9683742-1-2

1. Adult children of divorced parents—Psychology. 2. Divorce—Psychological aspects. I. Title.
HQ777.5L44 2001   306.89 C00-911593-5

Cover photo: Chris Stambaugh, Stambaugh Photographics, Edmonton, AB, Canada
Cover concept: Kevin Nienhuis
Cover production: Screaming Colour Inc.

Note: Some names have been changed to protect the privacy of friends and family members.

Inspire Media Inc.
4 Hayden Place
St. Albert, Alberta
T8N 6V1
email: chleibel@telusplanet.net
www.withinachildsheart.com

1   2   3   4   5   05   04   03   02   01

PRINTED AND BOUND IN CANADA

To my wife Trina, who taught me to love and trust, and also to accept myself. Thank you for all of your help, support, and understanding. Thanks for being you! I couldn't have done it without you. You are my love!

To my daughter, Briana, and my son, Brett. You both fill my soul with love and happiness every day. You are truly little miracles. I love you both with all of my heart!

Table of Contents

Preface

Dear Friend,

I made a promise—a promise that brought me to tears, made me laugh, tore my heart open, and healed my soul. Before I started writing *Within a Child's Heart*, I decided that if I was going to write this book—really write it—it had to be real. It had to be a true expression of how I felt about my journey through my parents' divorce.

I stood in my bathroom, looking at my reflection in the mirror, feeling vulnerable as I made a promise to capture the essence of the intimate details of the emotions, hurt, losses, lessons, and triumphs that I endured when my parents divorced. By sharing pieces of myself and details of my true story with you in this book, I believe that together we can help heal our wounds, open our hearts, and find deeper meaning to our lives. My intention is for you to laugh, cry, and grow with me as you read this book. Ultimately, I hope to touch your heart and show you that we can all overcome adversity, rise above our own circumstances, and build a better life for our families and ourselves!

I have learned that life is about choice. We all have choices to make and those choices lay the foundation for the pathways we call our lives. However, making our choices is not always easy. Sometimes we are forced to make extremely difficult decisions because of an uncontrollable situation, such as when a child is caught in the middle of his parents' divorce. At such times, we need to look deeper into ourselves—reach inside to find the courage, strength, and character we need to make those choices. They won't always be the right decisions, but the more we choose to face and conquer our fears, the more wisdom we will find in our hearts!

It is a great honor for me to share parts of my life with you through this book, and I thank you for allowing me the opportunity to do so. I commend all of you who face the obstacles that divorce brings and I honor you for your courage to survive and prosper! It is my belief that…

Great wisdom comes from great lessons of the heart!

Craig Henry Leibel

Acknowledgements

There are so many great people I want to thank and acknowledge— people who have helped me along the way, provided encouragement, and supported my purpose in writing this book. These people have taught me many life lessons, touched my soul, and inspired my work. It overwhelms me with gratitude to think of how blessed I am to have so many dynamic people in my life.

To Mom, Dad, and my brother Wes, writing this book has been a tremendous journey for us all. I thank you from the bottom of my heart for your support, your understanding, your love, the life gifts you gave me, and for being there when I needed you. Thank you for your encouragement and insights, and for lifting me up when I needed the boost. Most of all, thank you for supporting my decision to share parts of our family's history. It has been an incredible healing journey for me. I love you all.

I would like to give my Grandma Leibel special thanks for supporting and encouraging my ventures over the years and being there for me when I needed it. Thanks, Grandma. I love you.

As there are so many other people to name in my family, I would like instead to give all of my family special thanks and extend my appreciation for their support and kindness over the years. To everyone: Thanks.

Also, I wish to extend a special thank you to my wife's family, all of whom made me feel welcomed and like I was a part of their family—especially my mother- and father-in-law, Paul and Sally Casavant, and my sisters-in-law, Nicole and Tammy. You have all been tremendous over the years and I thank you for supporting my ambition and putting up with me.

I asked other adult children of divorce to share a meaningful message in the form of a quote, and these are included at the beginning of each chapter. These are messages from their hearts, life thoughts that they wanted to tell others who are struggling through the divorce journey. Thanks to Lynda McDonell, Jeff Ivanochko, Darren McKenna, Joanne Keylor, Celine Sirois, Kate Rogers, Wesley Mark Leibel, Darin Kowalchuk, Keith Sanheim, Michelle Keylor, and Peri Price for your words of wisdom in celebrating our survival and triumph.

I would like to express my appreciation to Rob Tanner and Robert Kroetsch for their guidance, encouragement, and support along the way. As well, I would like to give special acknowledgement to all the people who helped make a difference in the creation of this book. Much appreciation and special thanks to Christine Savage, Ruth Linka, Nathan Koll, Darren Pohl, Kevin Nienhuis, and Chris and Darlene Stambaugh.

Special appreciation to Jeff Ronaghan, Kate Rogers, Maryanne Gibson, Nathalie Clarke and Earl Shindruk, for their hard work, countless hours, commitment, and support to help launch the book.

Special thanks to Brenda Johnson for her support of the book and its vision. I would like to acknowledge Brenda for the incredible work that she does with the Rainbows Program, a non-profit organization that helps children grieve the loss of a parent through either death or divorce. It's an incredible program that helps thousands of children all over the world. Brenda heads up hundreds of Alberta volunteers who give their time and commitment to help children through a traumatic time. I honor and congratulate Brenda and all of the volunteers affiliated with the Rainbow Program. They are truly angels.

Special thanks to the self-proclaimed "unpaid consultant" D.S. (Del) Schjefte. Thanks for your encouragement and for lending your ear when I needed it. To Ken Charuk, thanks for everything.

And to all of my friends, I thank you for being a friend! To everyone else, thank you.

"I looked to blame someone for the breakup of my family, until I came to understand my parents' courage and their need for happiness. I realized that happiness can be found in many ways and we all deserve to be happy."

~Peri Price

Introduction

With one clean swoop, everything I had known became uncertain. I stood at the crossroads that my parents' divorce brought me to and felt confused, not knowing what the journey I was about to embark on would bring. It would be about life—about hurt, loss, heartache, courage, and triumph.

As children of divorce, we all have our own unique paths to walk and experiences to face. With the enormous changes divorce brings into our lives, we are all challenged by different situations and fears. Divorce adds many different variables into one's life, depending on a person's age, maturity, culture, history, and individual circumstances. However, at the same time, we all share a universal bond that links us together through the pain of losing our family.

Child, teenager, parent, friend, or relative—the impact of divorce touches us all. It has become a booming statistic. Unfortunately, somewhere in the evolution of family life, divorce has become a growing reality. It plays an astronomical role in our society, dramatically affecting hundreds of thousands of families all over the world. It has become so commonplace that many people choose to ignore the depth of the pain it creates in the lives of parents and children, downplaying the issue without recognizing that people need to grieve and heal over time. In reality, many children, teens, and adult children of divorce are left in pain, trying to convince themselves it doesn't hurt for fear of something being wrong with them. I believe there is a need to heal.

My parents' divorce was literally a life-altering experience for me. Even today, I continue to deal with new issues that arise or unresolved issues that I finally have the courage to tackle. The obstacles I faced were gigantic at times—sometimes absolutely unbearable.

They have continued to occur, from the day I was told about the divorce right through to today. I still find myself sifting through some of the lingering issues.

It has been a lifelong battle, and yet there is a positive side. The divorce experience helped me unravel truth upon truth. I know for certain that had the divorce not occurred, I would not be the person I am today. I am now equipped with better coping tools, a stronger heart, maturity, and the understanding to deal with situations in my life. It is the strength that we find within our hearts that builds character and wisdom in us all.

Within a Child's Heart is written from my heart, and it tells about my journey through my parents' divorce. It has become a doorway for my family and me to help us heal our wounds. Although it will never mend all of my wounds, it is a beginning to my journey to heal.

It is my hope that this book will provide you with useful insights and some understanding, and that it will support, inspire, educate, entertain, and encourage you to open your heart to your life, your family, and yourself.

CHAPTER ONE

Shock

"Life comes to those who bring themselves to life!"
~Craig Henry Leibel

I was fifteen years old when my parents sat my brother and me down at our kitchen table. I was sitting quietly with my eyes glazed over, as I wanted to phone my girlfriend instead of sitting through what I thought would be another of my parents' long-winded lectures on life. Being fifteen, I was convinced that I already knew all of the answers to life's mysteries.

It was January 2,1988—thirteen years ago. School was out for Christmas break and my family had just returned home from celebrating New Year's Eve at my grandma's lake cabin. Already suspicious of my parents' motives and the possible lecture about to occur, I began to wonder if perhaps my brother and I were going to be asked to take an oath on some favorable New Year's resolutions my parents had planned. However, that's not what happened. Not by a long shot.

What did happen was something I never, in my wildest dreams, thought would or could ever happen to me. It changed my life completely! It felt like watching the late news on television, hearing about all of the awful, head-shaking tragedies that happen every day but that you never really, truly believe could happen to you.

That's when my mom and dad looked us straight in the eyes, hesitated for a moment, and then dropped the bomb: They were splitting up!

An uncomfortable silence filled the room when my parents made their announcement. I didn't know exactly what I thought or felt in that moment, and I still don't know today. I just remember sitting there, dumbfounded in disbelief, trying to control this incredible urge to start laughing—not knowing whether or not they were joking. I looked around the table—at my mom, my dad, and then my twelve-year-old brother, Wes. I figured Wes was as surprised as I was, due to the indescribable expression on his face. He seemed to be thinking of the obvious question that was biting the tips of our tongues—but that we were both too scared to ask: Why? As I wondered what everyone at the table was thinking, I looked back at my parents and realized they weren't kidding. They were serious! Seeing my parents' faces, eagerly looking for some kind of response from us, overwhelmed me. A strange ache attacked my stomach, dropped to my toes, and suddenly shot back up through my legs, racing into my fingertips!

At that moment, I was completely numb. My mind was empty, lost. I couldn't think; I could barely breathe. I felt paralyzed. It couldn't be real. No way—not my parents! I couldn't believe it. All I could feel was that immense ache in the pit of my stomach, ready to burst out of my chest. My heart was beating so fast. I was stunned, totally shocked! I didn't know it at the time, but that instant—that one moment—would change my life, my brother's life, and my family … forever!

I know my brother felt the shock as I did, for we both sat there in silence—listening, not knowing if it was our place to say something, to get mad, to leave, to say it was okay, or to ask, "Why?" We just listened, not really absorbing anything, as our parents continued to explain the situation.

It was Mom's decision to leave. She explained that over the last few years, she and Dad had grown apart for various reasons and felt they needed some time to think things through and come to a decision about their relationship. My mom proposed a three-month trial separation. Her idea was that she and us kids would move out somewhere close to our home, and my parents would go to counseling sessions and attempt to work things out.

After my parents were finished talking, they asked us if we were okay. Although I appreciated their concern, I thought it was a ridiculous question, as I was feeling like a stick of dynamite they had just ignited! Totally lost for words, all I could say was, "Yeah, I'll be okay," as I ran up to my room, wondering what in the heck just happened. My parents were splitting up and it seemed that I was supposed to be just fine with that! I didn't know what was going to happen, let alone whether or not I would be okay.

I got into my room, shut the door, and sat on my bed. A river of emotions began to flood my mind. I contemplated, while staring at a poster on my wall, for over an hour. How could this have happened? Why was it happening? Was it something I did or didn't do? What did Dad do that would make Mom want to leave? What the heck did "growing apart" mean, anyway? It sounded like some kind of shrink babble to me. Did my mom do something wrong? They hardly ever fought. What was going on that I didn't know about? Was my dad seeing another woman? Was it money problems? Didn't my parents want to be a family? What would happen to us? Why did Mom want to leave? What could the problem be? What was I going to tell everyone? Would they really split up? What could I do? What did my brother think? What would my family say? Were we going to be okay? At that point, I felt mad—really mad!

I had to get out of the house. I wanted to be alone for awhile, to forget about what just happened. My mom insisted that we talk about it and asked me not to go, but I left anyway. As if I was going to listen to her, after that big news! I couldn't face my parents, plus I didn't want to be at home that night. I wasn't exactly sure where I was going, but it didn't really matter as long as it was somewhere other than my house.

We lived in a small town with a population of about three, maybe four thousand people. Therefore, like in most small towns, we knew almost everyone that lived there and they knew us. I couldn't help but think of all the gossip I was sure would fly around the town about my family now! They probably already knew. I just cringed at the thought of it. Our town was famous for its big hill with the Catholic Church standing impressively at the top, intersecting the heart of the town.

I left my house feeling so overwhelmed, that all I could do was run. I ran as hard and as fast as I could, through the snow and up the pathway leading to the big hill, where my family used to go tobogganing every Christmas. I ran faster and faster until finally I collapsed, exhausted, in front of the church. I leaned back, smelling the fresh night air, which felt cool on my face as I caught my breath. As I looked up to the sky, I tried to forget about all of the questions running through my mind, but I couldn't stop thinking. I had never felt like this before. My mouth wanted to scream, but nothing came out. I could only stare at the moon and the stars, asking, "Why? Why? Why?"

Soon, without finding an answer, I picked myself up and started walking aimlessly. I wandered around the town, ending up at the local arena, where I watched a peewee hockey game. I was a hockey player myself, actually—a good hockey player. Hockey was my love! My dream! All I ever wanted in my fifteen years of life was to be an NHL superstar. A day didn't go by where I wouldn't fantasize about playing with the greats, like Wayne Gretzky, Mark Messier, and Mario Lemieux. I would picture myself gripping the Stanley Cup in my hands, holding it high above my head as I paraded across the ice with my team in victory. How sweet it would be—winning the ultimate prize, playing in front of a sell-out crowd that was screaming and cheering!

Watching hockey helped to soothe and calm my emotions for a while. There were about ten minutes left in the second period of the game, and the home team scored! The crowd cheered as that goal tied up the score. The goal triggered some memories about Wes and me playing hockey with Dad in the basement. We would play and practice for hours on end. I began thinking about our favorite game—the shootout. Dad would put the pads on and play goal as Wes and I took turns shooting to see who could score the most goals. The highlight of the game always came when my dad took a fierce, well-executed slapshot right in the family jewels! Laughter would echo throughout the basement. Boy, Wes and I would laugh and laugh! I don't know exactly why, but it didn't matter how many times it happened; it was always funny. I guess you could say it's kind of a male-bonding ritual.

Our basement came alive when we heard the words "Game on!" and the speakers of the ghetto blaster roared out our favorite hockey song, "I Wanna Rock!" This was followed, of course, by Mom hollering at us, "Turn it down!" Most of the time, we played for an hour or so and then the gloves would fly across the room and the real battle would begin. I guess brotherly love only lasts so long when you're in an intense game of floor hockey. Punches were exchanged and I often stood victorious, being the older brother. (However, today it might be a different story, as my little brother is not so little anymore. He tends to regularly remind me of that fact.) Generally, it would be a short fight and then a half-hour later, we would be back to playing.

Wes and I had so much fun together. I wondered if all of that would change now because of the breakup. I could feel some tears building up in my eyes. Then all of a sudden, the home team scored again and the crowd cheered! Their cheers startled me enough that I was able to regain my composure.

I tried to continue watching hockey, but questions about the separation began to consume me. I couldn't believe my parents were seriously splitting up. As hard as I tried to figure out what could have caused this to happen, I just couldn't think of anything. I had always thought of my parents as a happy couple who were very much in love. I rarely saw them fight, and when they did, it never lasted very long. They would make up and go on as though that was the end of it—at least, it seemed that way in my mind. Most of my memories of their relationship are of them laughing and having a good time together. Typically, they shared the same spontaneous sense of fun.

One instance in particular stands out in my mind. It was early one Sunday morning and Dad had just finished cooking pancakes. My dad always cooked his so-called 'famous' fluffy pancakes every Saturday and Sunday morning for our pancake-eating challenge. The competition wasn't even just between Wes and me. My dad, along with some of my uncles, included my cousins in the challenge, too. Every weekend, out came the pancakes and we would stuff ourselves silly, each of us trying to beat the record and become the Ultimate Pancake-Eating Champion! My brother held the record at twenty-two—most of which were silver-dollar pancakes, but we gave the title to him anyway, seeing that he couldn't walk for a few hours afterward. I was so sick of eating pancakes that I tried to boycott by taking an oath never to eat them again! I hoped that this would express to Dad my desire for something new to eat. I personally think the whole thing was a conspiracy between my uncles and my dad so they wouldn't have to learn to cook anything else.

Mom, who had been an aerobics instructor for a few years, was practicing her dance routine in the house as my dad cooked away. She had the music on and was testing out some new steps. Once the last silver-dollar pancake was claimed by my brother, Dad decided to join Mom in her routine by adding some of his own uniquely patented moves. I could not believe it! It looked as though he was on a mission to invent a whole new kind of aerobics—a cross between the newest dance craze, called breakdancing, mixed in with a little of the jitterbug and what looked to be a form of ballroom dancing! Mom really got into it with him, adding her own moves, which Dad then tried to copy. Mom kept making each new move a little faster and more difficult for him to follow. They were laughing and having a great time when suddenly Dad jumped in the air, going for the spectacular finale—only to land hard, buckling his ankle. Down he went. You could hear the ten-count ring throughout the house! Although he was quite hurt, the whole family could not stop laughing! I must admit it was one of the funnier things I have ever seen in my life. We had to rush my dad to the hospital and he ended up on crutches, with a hairline fracture in his ankle. It took everything my mom had not to burst out laughing when the doctor asked, "Well, what have we here?"

My parents always seemed to have so much fun together. We all did as a family. I just could not understand what the problem was. They said they had grown apart, but I really didn't know what that meant. I wanted facts! Not something that sounded like psychobabble, but hard-core data and sound reasoning. I wanted to know the truth, no matter what it was, and I wanted to know it now! When I think about it, though, I don't know if I would have been able to handle any more at that moment.

The second-period buzzer sounded in the hockey game and brought me out of my trance. For a minute, I actually forgot I was sitting up in the stands of the arena. I looked over towards the doors, considering going to the concession for a drink, when I saw two of my school friends, Kyle and Dean, coming up the stairs. I quickly turned away, hoping they hadn't spotted me. I began to feel scared and nervous. I desperately hoped they wouldn't come over. I didn't want to talk to anyone. I was confused and I felt all tongue-tied. What would I say? Sure enough, before I had time to sneak out the back way, they spotted me and waved. They came over, sat down, and said, "Hi Craig, how's it going?" At first, I tried to keep cool and pretend everything was great, thinking that I didn't have to tell them anything. But they sensed something was bothering me and Kyle asked, "What's wrong? You look like you've seen a ghost or something. Are you sick?" I wasn't sure if it was the sweat on my forehead, sliding down my cheek, or my bloodshot eyes that gave me away. I desperately wanted to hide, but even though I was embarrassed, I just couldn't keep what I was feeling inside. It was too big. I blurted out, "I'm pissed off and am just trying to get some air." They asked, "Why?" and the words came out as if I had lost control of my mouth: "My parents just told me they are splitting up."

At first, neither of my friends spoke. They simply looked at me, very puzzled. I thought that maybe I shouldn't have said anything. The air started to feel like it was squeezing around me when out of nowhere, Kyle said, "Hey, don't worry about it. My real parents are divorced too. They have been for years." I looked at him, confused because I thought that he lived with both of his real parents. He explained that his mom had remarried. That cleared up some questions I had about his family but never really understood or asked about before. I wasn't sure if I was intruding, but I had to ask Kyle, "Why did your parents divorce? Were you shocked when they told you?" He offered to talk about it, explaining that his parents had split up a long time ago when he was about four years old, and he didn't remember much about it, but that he felt it was for the better. Without going into great detail, he said his dad wasn't very good to his mom, so she left. He hadn't seen his dad for quite some time and I could tell that hurt him deeply. I said I was sorry that happened to him because, at that moment, I understood. I understood the pain and hurt he had been carrying around for all of those years.

I felt a strong connection with Kyle that night. We talked a little while longer about divorce and our families. Soon, Dean joined the conversation. Ironically, his parents were also divorced. He said he wasn't surprised at all that his parents had divorced, explaining that "all they ever did was fight." He said it was too bad that it had to be that way, but at least it was more peaceful with them apart. Our discussion became very overwhelming, so we soon changed the subject and enjoyed watching the hockey game together.

I am really glad I got a chance to talk to my friends that night, as scary and as awkward as it felt. I hadn't known what to say or how they would react and what they would think about me, but they just listened and I got to listen to them. I didn't feel as alone anymore, which felt good, but I was still very confused and wondered what would happen to my family now. I left the arena feeling scared, but less alone than I did going in. After talking with my friends about their experiences, I knew that somehow I would survive.

Walking out of the arena, I was feeling better. I thought that maybe I could seek comfort from some of my other friends, Dwayne and Kelsey, as well. I saw them through their front window and they waved for me to come over. They were surprised to see me, and Dwayne asked, "Hi Craig, what are you doing strolling around in the night?" Feeling more comfortable after talking with Kyle and Dean, I told them I had some bad news. They asked what was wrong, so I proceeded to tell them, "My parents just told me they are splitting up." They both seemed shocked, exclaiming, "Your parents? No way!" I wasn't quite sure what I was waiting for them to say as I stood there, but I started to feel very uncomfortable. All they could ask was, "Why?" Exactly my question! Since I didn't really know myself, I found it hard to give them any kind of an explanation, so I said nothing, despite their questioning. Needless to say, I didn't find the comfort I was looking for and the conversation became difficult, so I left. I realized that I was obviously going to experience many different reactions. At the time, I felt hurt by how these friends forgot about me and instead simply carried on about how shocked and confused they were about my parents. Later, though, I learned that we can't expect people to know just what to say or do. All we can do is ask for them to listen.

My mom was still awake when I arrived home. She was sitting on the couch in the living room, waiting for me. I didn't feel like talking to her, but I could sense that she needed to know I was okay. She asked, "How are you?" A rush of anxiety filled my body when she spoke. Speechless, I began to tense and all I could say was, "I'm okay. I just needed to be alone," as I walked up the stairs to my room.

The stars were really shining in the night sky. I stretched out on my bed, watching them glisten through my bedroom window. My thoughts scattered like a pinball. I wondered how many stars I would have to wish upon just to erase this day and have my family stay together. What would it take? As much as I tried to fall asleep, I couldn't stop my mind from racing. I felt a river of emotions, and questions kept appearing like visions. What's going to happen now? Where is my mom going to live? Why is my dad not doing something? Why is he letting her go? Are we still going to do things as a family? Then I remembered that they had said it was only going to be for three months—so maybe, just maybe, it would work itself out. What if it didn't? A little tear slid down my cheek and I finally fell asleep.

The Next Day

The morning came very slowly and I felt terrible. I had hardly slept. I went downstairs, hoping the whole thing had been a bad nightmare. My dad was in the kitchen—cooking pancakes, of course—and my mom was in the living room, dusting the bookshelf. It was as if nothing had happened, except for the eerie silence lingering everywhere in the house. The calm before the storm is the best way to describe it. It felt like watching a horror movie as the music slowly builds up before the killer jumps out to claim his victim. The entire day continued with very little conversation and an awkward feeling for all of us. We basically did our own thing, keeping to ourselves, watching eagerly to see what the others would do next. I didn't like it. I didn't like it at all. It felt like a stupid game of musical chairs.

As the sun went down and the night drew closer, I was feeling very uncomfortable because no one was saying anything. I decided to leave again. I couldn't take the unbearable silence; I wasn't used to it. We were always so busy, and now … nothing. As I walked out, I slammed the door. *Smash!* I was looking for any attention I could get. Dad yelled, "Craig, come here! I want to talk to you." I kept walking until he came outside and said, "Craig, now! Please." I stopped beside the car in the driveway, opened the door, and crawled in. My dad followed me, abruptly opened the driver's door, and climbed in.

He opened the conversation by asking, "How are you doing with all of this?" I didn't know what to say. From the explanation I was given, it seemed that it was Mom's decision to leave, and I wasn't sure why Dad was going along with it. I wanted to know why he was not putting up a fight or doing something to stop it. A little nervous, but more angry, I blurted out, "Dad, why are you letting Mom leave? What did you do?" He paused for awhile, trying to find some words, and then said, "Son, you need to understand some things. Your mom and I have some problems with our relationship and we need to work them out. Your mom feels we need some space in order to do that. Things haven't been very good between us for awhile and we want to try to make them better, for us and for our family."

To me, it sounded like too political of an answer, so I questioned further: "Why does Mom have to leave in order to do that?" I don't know if my dad really knew the answer to that. He stared forward for awhile before saying, "Craig, at this point, I know I need to give your mom her space if we are going to get through this. The whole thing is between your mom and me, and I want you to know that it's not about you or your brother. We love you both. It's nobody's fault. If your mom and I can change it, we will do everything in our power to do so." I could tell my dad was devastated. Whatever had happened between them, he obviously never expected Mom to leave. All he could tell me was that he didn't want it to be like this and that they would work out what they needed to in time. He asked me to give them time. I felt like he was hiding some facts, but I could tell nothing more was going to be said. I agreed to my dad's request and we went back into the house.

After I talked to Dad, I felt better about the arrangement and was more positive about the idea of my parents working things out in counseling. After all, three months was a short time. I could live through it if that's what it was going to take. I wanted to help too, so I devised a plan in my head that I thought would contribute. My plan was simple. I would help out with chores around the house, not fight with my brother, and try to give my parents some time to themselves by staying out of their way as best as I could. I figured the more chance they had to talk and be together, the faster they could work things out.

For the rest of the week I was on my best behavior. Mom had not yet moved out, and sometimes there were traces of laughter between my parents. I was beginning to believe that my parents deciding to split up was a temporary situation. I hoped my mom might just stay and forget about the whole three-month-trial idea.

It wasn't until the end of the week that my over-eager hope changed into suspicion. I needed to use the phone to call my girl-friend. I had told her about the proposed breakup, and she too was very upset over the news. I thought she would welcome my positive attitude. I had promised her that I would call and let her know how things were going. I thought it was looking promising and I was a lit-tle excited. I couldn't wait to tell her; I needed to tell someone. However, my dad was on the phone talking with some of my relatives and my grandma. He was literally on the phone all night. I told him many times that I needed to use the phone, to the point where I eventually informed him it was a life-and-death emergency! I wasn't lying; it really felt like it was. At fifteen years old, my whole relation-ship with my girlfriend was based on the telephone! If I had to wait any longer, it would be too late to call and it would be straight to the doghouse for me.

Every fifteen minutes, I walked down the flight of stairs to the kitchen to see if my dad was still on the phone. Then I headed back to my room to pace impatiently beside my bed, until I couldn't wait anymore and had to go down and check again. By about the seventh time that I went to check, Dad lost his patience. He told the person on the phone that he would call back and shouted to me, "Go to your room, now!" I thought, *Oh shoot, I am going to get it!* I hurried to my room, waiting unwillingly. The door flew open and my dad came bursting into the room, shouting, "Craig, sit down!" He scared the heck out of me. He said, "Son, I know you need the phone, but I am talking with the counselor right now." The butterflies in my stomach started their formation as I listened to Dad explain that Mom had found a place and planned to move out in two days. He also told me that they had announced the trial separation to everyone in the family. All I could do was apologize to my dad, and he just nodded. He put his hands on his knees and sat on my bed as he sighed. He looked over at me and said he still needed to use the phone and that I would have to wait until tomorrow. Then he left.

Every hope I had built up exploded in that moment. It hit me hard! It was the first time I really felt that the separation was going to be a reality. I flopped down on my bed and wiped the tears on my pillow as I forced myself to sleep.

Two days later, Mom moved out. I didn't want to be there when she moved, so Wes and I went to stay with one of our cousins. We always had a blast when we stayed with our cousins or when they stayed with us at our house. We stayed there for a few days, playing hockey, relaxing in their hot tub, joking around with some of their friends, venturing outside, and even taking their parents' car for a spin around the block, which my cousin took the heat for later! It was a good time, but even in all of our fun, every now and then my emotions would sneak up, reminding me of the situation we had to go back to. I just wanted to pretend nothing had happened—to avoid having to face the truth.

When the fun was over, it was time to go home, time to face my mom being gone. I was mad, upset, and scared. I didn't want to leave my cousins and deal with the reality that my parents were splitting up. On the ride home, I sat quietly, wondering what tomorrow would bring. I had no answers, and I was definitely not prepared for the extraordinary changes that were about to take place in my life!

It's Over!

My parents called a family meeting. At this point, they had been separated for about three weeks and had attended a few counseling sessions to work out some of their differences. I was not exactly sure what the meeting was for. I hoped they had resolved some of their problems and were planning to end the separation. I went there thinking positively about the possibility that my parents did in fact reconcile some differences. After all, it was not even close to three months yet and we were already having a family meeting! The meeting was held at my mom's new house. Therefore, despite my hopefulness, my instincts were telling me this wasn't about good news. I arrived by myself and joined my mom and my brother in the living room. The room was quiet. My mom and Wes were sitting across from each other, and the look on Mom's face told the story. Any and all hope I had salvaged came to a screeching halt! I could feel the butterflies fluttering in my stomach as I sat down next to my brother. My mom didn't say anything to either of us; she simply asked if we would like something to eat or drink.

I knew right then that this was it. My mom looked determined—like she had made a hard decision that she was uncomfortable with, but was going to follow through with rain or shine. Part of me felt very disappointed and concerned for my mom, but the other part was angry. It had only been three weeks since the breakup, and they had said there was going to be a three-month trial before any decisions were supposed to be made. The doorbell rang and my dad came into the living room. His expression didn't look much better. He said hello to Wes and me and sat down.

We all sat in the living room, waiting for someone to open the conversation. I looked over at my brother to see what his take on this was. I could tell he was feeling uncomfortable. He looked worried, too. I hated the silence! It got into my head and felt like a hammer was pounding down on my heart with every beat! I was anxious to learn about the purpose of the meeting, yet I really didn't want to hear what I knew was coming.

Finally, Mom broke the silence, opening the conversation by getting straight to the point. She informed Wes and me that the reason our parents had called the meeting was because they had gone to some counseling sessions and reached a decision. I was starting to prepare for the big bomb. My body was shaking and I was on the edge of my seat, waiting for the verdict—just in case it was good news. Mom's voice crackled as she said, sounding scared, "We have decided to keep the separation permanent." I quickly asked, "You mean like … forever?" She nodded her head, yes. I paused for a minute and looked over at Dad for some kind of guidance to this madness, but he just nodded his head in agreement. I didn't feel anything. I was numb again. Son of a gun, I knew it! I knew this would be the case, but why? I was still in such shock over the whole thing that it didn't matter anymore. In a weird way, I felt it would have been worse if my mom had decided to come back, because it wouldn't have felt real. If she did, I knew it would be because of us kids, and that was not what I wanted. Somewhere in my heart, I knew there must have been a good reason, even if I didn't understand it.

My brother and I didn't say much. I was upset that my parents had decided it was over. However, what really made me mad was the fact they were supposed to go to counseling for three months and, in my mind, make a valiant effort to piece together what was missing. It hadn't even been a month! I felt like I was lied to and betrayed. Like somehow our family wasn't worth it. If they already knew this in the beginning, why didn't they just say it was going to be forever, instead of buttering us up for the kill? I felt like my parents were trying to make it easier on us or lessen the sting by giving us some hope with the whole 'trial' thing. However, in doing so, they just confused me more.

Listening to my mom go on about how things would be now was only getting me angrier and angrier. I couldn't believe it. She was describing how I was going to conduct myself and how I was going to live. Decisions I felt were mine to make were being tossed all over the living room. I couldn't stand it anymore, and I shouted, "Why, Mom? Why?"

She paused at my interruption and collected her thoughts. I waited patiently until she began to explain, "At our last counseling session, we were talking about a situation from our past when I was very hurt about an incident. As I told the counselor about it, your dad got mad and stormed out of the office, saying, "This happened over ten years ago and should have been dealt with then!" Mom continued, "As I always have, I started running after your father, because I felt guilty that I had upset him. The counselor stopped me and asked why I was running after him. I sat back down in the chair and finally realized that I had been running after him and feeling guilty for years and years, and my feelings were still not being heard. I made my decision right then; I knew it was over. I felt dead inside. I have never been heard, and I knew the only way I could continue was on my own."

"That's it? That's the reason?" I said, not fully understanding what my mom meant. She looked at me and said, "No, Craig, that's only one of many reasons. But yes, Craig, it is over!"

As I sat in silence, I wanted to know all the other reasons— exactly why this was happening to our family! Mom couldn't say anything more, and Dad could only give me the same sugar-coated story about growing apart and becoming two different people. I felt like he really didn't know what to say—almost as though he finally realized that he should have done something long before this. The explanations were definitely not good enough and I knew I wasn't going to get many more details, so I said, "I have only one more question. Do you still love each other?" My parents just looked at me, and my mom started to cry. I knew the answer was ultimately 'no'—although as I looked into my dad's face that night, his eyes spoke 'yes'. It just wasn't enough anymore. Dad ended the meeting by expressing their concern for my brother and me, asking if we were okay. Wes and I remained silent, because there was nothing we could say in that moment that wouldn't have hurt our parents. It was the last time we talked as a family.

There was no more denying it; it was definitely a reality. My parents had decided it was over. They were splitting up for good. I still couldn't believe it. My family was gone and it hurt! It felt like I had lost something so great that it was as if I had died. I didn't know what was going to happen. The marriage was over ... and the new beginning was shaping up to be the ultimate roller-coaster ride of my life.

What's Going to Happen Now?

I felt lost and helpless as I walked in the moonlight up the sidewalk to Mom's new home. This was my first visit to her house since she had declared the marriage was over. A month had gone by since our family meeting. I had really been missing her, but I was incredibly torn between being excited to see her and being hurt by what had happened. I didn't know if I was going to hug her or unleash my anger on her. I was so filled with heartache, confusion, and defeat about the breakup. I just couldn't allow myself to feel excited to be there.

I rang the doorbell and waited. I wasn't sure why I did that, but it didn't feel right just to walk in. It wasn't my house and I didn't live there. Even though Mom had a room for me, I had never been in it. The doorknob turned and she greeted me at the door, asking me to come in. I could see she wanted to put her arms around me and give me a big hug, but my instincts led me to shrug her off as I peeled off my coat and walked in. I really wanted to hug her, but I also wanted to yell at her about how much the separation hurt. Deciding to keep cool, I said hello to my brother, who was in the living room watching television. As I sat down on the couch next to him, Mom announced what she had made for supper—spaghetti and meatballs, my favorite.

I looked at Wes and we both smirked, because for a long time, we had played a little game between us every time we ate spaghetti and meatballs. We would each take turns coming up with new, special secret ingredients to add to the other's spaghetti without his knowledge. Then we would eat our meal and guess what the secret ingredients were. Once, Wes added Cheez Whiz, crushed jalapenos, and Tabasco sauce—practically a whole jar of it—to mine, knowing Dad wouldn't let us leave the table until we had finished every last bite on our plates. Wes still chuckles to himself when he thinks about watching me in excruciating pain, slowly swallowing super-hot spaghetti and drinking water by the jug, as Dad hung over my shoulder to make sure I ate every bite!

Needless to say, not much was said during dinner. It was mostly small talk about school. Halfway through, my brother and I gathered our plates and headed out to sit in front of the old thirteen-inch black-and-white television to watch some of the hockey game. Hockey Night in Canada. We loved it! Even in black and white. After we were finished eating and the game was in intermission, we quickly joined Mom in the kitchen to help finish cleaning up.

As I dried the dishes, Mom asked how I was doing. I said I was okay and that everything was fine, but really, I was ready to explode with anxiety. Inside, I was really hurting and felt like I couldn't stop it, but I didn't want Mom to know or be bothered with it. I felt like she had enough to deal with and I was embarrassed that I was having a hard time. Over the last few weeks, I had been trying hard to constantly occupy myself with something in order to avoid dealing with the hurt—until it became so overwhelming that I would have to make myself stop thinking altogether, blanking out my mind completely.

Mom, who could see right through me, again asked, "Craig, are you sure you're okay? You seem upset. It's alright if you are." Although I wanted to scream out, I couldn't. I didn't want to be a burden and I needed to feel like a man—like I could take it. I was scared to say anything. So many emotions were bottled up inside of me, and I felt like all the walls were crumbling down despite my efforts to hold them up. Mom continued the dishes in silence as she watched me dry. It seemed to go on forever, when she asked, "Is it that you don't want to talk to me? Are you mad at me? I really, really miss you, Craig."

Stunned and scared, I quickly said, "No." Without missing a beat, she asked, "I know your decision was no, but are you ever going to come and live with me?"

That was too much guilt, hurt, confusion, frustration, anger, sorrow, and helplessness all at once, ahhhhh…! A rush of tears burst from my eyes unexpectedly. I quickly retreated to the living room, and Mom followed me. I fought my emotions as best as I could, staring blankly at the television. Mom said, "It's okay to be upset, to be angry. Do you want to talk about it? Please, don't be afraid. I promise I will just listen." I walked back into the kitchen, trying to fight the emotions, but it was useless. Face to face with the cupboards, I tilted my head toward the floor and leaned on the countertop for support. Mom stood behind me, waiting. I whispered, "Mom, it hurts. It really hurts. I feel so helpless, like I am lost." She reached for my arm and hugged me, repeating, "It's okay. I'm so sorry. It's okay." I continued, "I don't know what's happening, who I am anymore, what I am a part of. Everything is different and I don't know why! Mom, you have no idea how much it hurts!"

As a tear slid down my cheek, I choked out a question. "Mom, what's going to happen now—are we going to be okay? I am so scared." She pulled me closer and held me tight as she cried for a minute or two and then, in a soft whisper, said, "I'm not sure what's going to happen or what lies ahead, but I promise you, Craig, we will be okay. We will get through it and take it one step at a time." It felt good to hear her say that, even though I didn't completely believe her. I asked, "How do I get rid of the pain, Mom? Sometimes it hurts so badly that I can't take it. It takes over and becomes too much. I don't know what to do."

Mom paused for a moment and then gave me a gift. A gift about life. She said, "Craig, when things get bad, or become so overwhelming that I am not sure what to do, I put it up to God." I asked what she meant. Mom continued, "I look to the heavens to talk to your grandfather and ask for help." Puzzled, I asked, "How do you do that?" She took my hands and told me to take all of the hurt, the questions, and the overwhelming feelings I was having, bunch them up, and ask God for his help and guidance. I could feel a weight lifting off my back as I did this. I started to feel like I didn't have to figure everything out in that one moment. I could take a deep breath and feel the stress ease. I had a powerful force looking out for me—a force to help me trust myself, and to give me faith and guide me to where I needed to go. Although I was still uncertain as to what the future would hold, I believed that God would provide.

It's Not My Fault

For a long time, I blamed my mom for the divorce. Mom made the decision. She was the one who chose to leave the family. It was her reasoning that sealed my parents' fate. Therefore, I held her responsible for the separation. I felt betrayed by her decision to leave before the three-month trial period was up. I had believed that my parents were going to make a valiant effort to work things out. Then, suddenly, it seemed to me that Mom gave up—threw in the towel like our family wasn't worth the effort I so desperately believed it was. Although I didn't understand and was completely shocked by their decision, I couldn't help feeling that there must be something I could do to fix this. To bring my parents back together. No matter how much it hurt or how much I wanted to fix it, and to change Mom's mind, the reality was that I couldn't say nor do anything. It was totally out of my control. Unwillingly at first, I had to accept that the breakup was about my parents and their relationship, and not about my brother or me.

Placing the blame on my mom clouded my judgment and deeply damaged our relationship, causing many more hurtful things to happen. In the beginning, I was so confused by my parents' reasoning and unable to answer the question of why, that it became easier to blame than to search for the truth. It took me a long time and many heated arguments with my parents to learn it wasn't just Mom's fault. In fact, it wasn't my mom's, my dad's, my brother's, my family's, or my fault. My parents' actions together created their marriage and ultimately, their actions together also created their divorce.

Mom and Dad were and still are both responsible for the divorce.

Divorce brings mountains of emotions, valleys of changes, and oceans of choices. With the explosive pace and immense transitions, placing blame becomes easy, almost like a form of survival. It becomes a way to avoid the truth in order to avoid the pain. However, as much as I initially placed the blame on my mom, many children from divorced families decide to blame themselves. They live with tremendous burdens, assuming responsibility and believing the divorce is happening because of them—something they did or didn't do, perhaps. Sometimes they worry that they are in the way because they aren't wanted. Some children might believe they aren't good enough or are unable to live up to their parents' expectations. For many unwarranted reasons, children may believe their parents' divorce is their fault. However, it is absolutely not true. Children are innocent!

From the first time I saw the photograph that I eventually chose for the cover of this book, it reached inside me and grabbed my heart. Intense emotions sailed through my body as I stared at the image. I could feel the innocence of the child. How truly fragile, pure, and innocent children really are. In the photograph, I saw myself—along with the many other children who are faced with adversity and challenges of the heart, unaware of the voyage that lies ahead. It doesn't matter what their age, sex, ethnic background, education, or financial status is. It doesn't matter whether or not the children saw their parents' divorce coming or perhaps even wanted the divorce to happen—it is never their fault! The children didn't cause it, and they can't fix it. It's not their responsibility. Their only responsibility is just to be children.

CHAPTER TWO

Change

"When life gets us down, oftentimes we focus only on the sorrow. We don't look ahead to see that the healing light at the end of the tunnel is always shining upon us."

~Lynda McDonell

Even before we had the family meeting at which Mom declared my parents' marriage to be over, I was faced with one of the biggest decisions of my life: Where do I live?

The house was empty. Wes and I had arrived home late in the evening from my cousins' house and no one was home. Mom had just moved out, and the three-month trial separation had begun. It was time to face the fact that she had left. I tried hard to deny it, but it was no use. Eventually, I would have to face the inevitable truth.

Shortly after my uncle and cousins dropped Wes and me off, Mom arrived to pick us up. She had moved into a small duplex located nearby, and she was prepared to take both of us there to live with her. Wes decided to go, but I just couldn't. From out of nowhere, when Mom asked if we were ready to depart, I refused. I told her I was going to stay. Surprised, she protested. However, I insisted that it was what I wanted to do. I didn't know exactly why; I just knew I needed to stay and wait for my dad. I was far from ready to accept that the separation was becoming a reality, so I wasn't going to act like it was. Plus, all of my stuff was in my room upstairs. It was my home.

As I waited for Dad, I stood in the middle of the kitchen, listening to the still air. All I could hear was the sound of the clock's hands moving every time a second went by. Tick. Tick. Tick. All the lights were out and I began to walk slowly through the house. Through the front bay window, I could see the moon shining in the night sky. I walked over to the window, leaning my forehead on the cool glass as I stood staring at the stars, looking for answers and comfort. I asked myself over and over again, "Why does it have to be this way? Why did Mom leave? What's happening to our family?" I felt that there must be something that could be done to change the situation.

Dad was supposed to be home any minute, but as usual, he was running late. I was getting very anxious. I felt numb, and my mind kept running the same questions over and over. It was a feeling I had never felt before. I didn't like it. I didn't like it at all! A hollow, achy sensation tingled all over my body and the more I tried to fight it, the more it scared me.

Feeling desperate, I continued to stare at the stars and the mystical shape of the moon. I had been denying the fact that my parents were breaking up, holding onto the hope they would work it out. Up until this point, I never allowed myself to truly believe Mom would move out. But now she was gone! I was alone in the house, and for the first time in my life, I felt empty. My spirit was torn. I let out a loud sigh and I could feel how nervous I was, almost shaking. A symphony of emotions sang out inside me. I felt petrified, upset, confused, disillusioned, tired, out of control, pissed off, depressed, lost, sad, and lonely—all at the same time. It was as if I was a volcano preparing to erupt. My body paralyzed, I felt the rush of anxiety explode into tears. I could not contain myself. I couldn't fight it; it was just too much to handle. All I could do was cry and cry. I cried for a long time, feeling more alone in that moment than I ever had before in my entire life.

I felt so many things. Everything was changing. I was angry with Mom because, as I saw it, she had walked out on the family. I was mad at Dad for upsetting Mom to the point where she decided to leave. I was mad at myself because I couldn't do anything to fix it. It felt like my whole life had been a lie—like the years prior were somehow no longer real. Like they didn't mean anything. I was still in shock and scared of what life would be like now. What would change? How could we ever still be a family? Everything I had known while growing up, all the memories—would they change too?

I could see headlights in the driveway as my dad drove up. When he came into the house, we didn't talk. He seemed lost, like he had been blind-sided by a freight train he never saw coming. I wanted to ask him why the separation really happened—to ask him what he did wrong, and scream at him for letting Mom leave. Instead, we both sat in the living room all night in silence.

The next morning, the phone rang. Mom was calling to again ask if I would go stay with her and Wes. It was one of the most difficult decisions I ever had to make, and it was a question that I felt was unfair to have to answer. Where do you want to live—with your mom or your dad? Mom wanted Wes and me to go live with her, but Dad wanted us to live with him. I couldn't decide. I loved both of my parents and there was no good reason for me to choose one over the other. I was old enough to make my own decision, but how could I choose between my parents? I decided I couldn't. Therefore, instead of deciding to live with either parent, I was going to decide what was right for me. It was the only sane thing I thought possible.

I was not in support of my mom's decision to leave the family, and I felt I needed to make a stand for what I believed in, and that was my family. I needed to find the truth. I needed to make sense of what was happening and I wasn't prepared for how rapidly every thing was changing. I needed to hang on to as much as I could. I made my stand and unfortunately, Mom took the brunt of it.

Our phone conversation became very heated as I said, "I'm not going to move in with you, Mom. I'm going to stay in our family's house with Dad." She paused for a while and then, with sadness in her voice, asked, "Why?" I tried to explain my reasoning, but she interrupted, asking if I was punishing her. I got mad because she interrupted me, so I shouted, "Mom, how am I supposed to decide where I should live? How can I pick? Who do I pick? Why should I even have to decide this? It's insane!" I was livid and I was not going to choose one or the other! I explained that I felt Mom's choice to leave was also her choice to leave the family. Moving out of the house was the next step. I told her that since I wanted to keep the family together, I had decided to stay home with Dad. I wanted to hold onto what I believed in.

Mom shouted at me, "What do you want me to do, Craig? Do you want me to go back? If that's what you want, if that's how it has to be, I will!" For a minute, I thought, *This is my chance! All I have to do is say the word and Mom will come home. What's the catch?* I was just about to say, "Yes, please come back," when I stopped. I could hear the crackle in Mom's voice through the phone, and I just couldn't say it. My brain was saying, *Craig, you dumb fool! What are you waiting for? Say the words.* But my heart was saying something very different. I could sense my mom's fear and guilt. Although I didn't understand, somewhere inside I knew it wouldn't be right, and I found myself saying, "No, Mom, I don't want you to come back." A single tear slid down my cheek as I heard her say, "Craig, I am sorry. I am so sorry."

The conversation went silent for a long while. I was feeling guilty about hurting my mom by not going to live with her, but I still had to do what was right for me. I had no more to say, so I asked Mom if she would be okay. With a broken tone, she said softly, "I'll be okay … it's … okay."

Mom was very upset with my decision, but she honored it. I believe she felt it was my way of punishing her for hurting me, and maybe it was. However, my real purpose was to make my parents see that our family was the most important thing and I didn't want it to be taken away. It was all I could do to hold on to what I loved, even though it hurt to do it.

Wes, on the other hand, decided to live with Mom. He didn't want her to be alone, and he knew I was going to live with Dad. I respected him for that, but at the same time, my parents' split caused me to lose my brother, too. That really hurt. As much as we fought and got on each other's nerves, I loved my brother. Not having him around left a gaping hole in my heart. I missed him terribly. It's funny how you never truly realize how important people are to you until they're gone in some form. I learned very quickly about some important things that I had taken for granted before the divorce. After Wes moved in with Mom, we still spent time together once and awhile, mostly at family events, but it was never the same. We didn't have the same spirit we once had. All those days of playing hockey in the basement and jumping on the trampoline in the back yard disappeared.

Over the years, I learned how important it is to stay in touch with my brother—to make the effort to set time aside to do things together and stay connected. As brothers, all we have is each other. He's a great guy!

Deciding to live with Dad in our family home was the first of a multitude of changes I could never have imagined. Everything I had known about my family, my friends, relationships, family functions, birthdays, Christmas, and the rest of my life—it was all about to … change!

Loss of the Family

The family I knew, loved, belonged to, and was proud of—the family I called mine—was gone! After the announcement that the separation was permanent, divorce was inevitable. My family died. The family unit was gone, leaving me scrambling to redefine what my family was and meant.

How I longed for all of the little things in life that I had been taking for granted. I hadn't realized how important they really were to me. The one thing I missed the most was eating with my family—sitting down at the supper table at 6:00 PM with Wes, Mom, and Dad. We would discuss our day, our thoughts, and plans for the days to follow—talking, laughing, and having fun while we ate. I regret all the times Wes and I would try to sneak off and sit in front of the television to watch "Three's Company" instead of staying at the supper table. I secretly had a crush on Suzanne Somers and just couldn't miss the show. Now I would give anything for one more dinner with my family, like it used to be.

I missed things like watching Dad and Mom hug each other when they got home from work, planning summer vacations, weekend outings as a family, going over my report card with my parents, watching sporting events together, enjoying activities like slow-pitch baseball with my parents, listening to Mom and Dad plan for the future, and even cleaning the house every other Saturday as a family. Now all of that had changed. Everything became different, and most of the fun was no longer existent. My attitude and behavior became so serious, as did Mom and Dad's. We talked without smiling and lived with a sense of caution.

Even the simple things—like making a bowl of popcorn, renting a movie, and watching it together as a family—were gone. There was something about watching a movie with my whole family that made me feel good. The atmosphere was very comforting. Everyone got a blanket—except Dad, even though he was the one who needed it the most because he would fall asleep within the first half-hour, taking up the whole couch so that everyone else had to sit on the floor. We would all share a huge bowl of popcorn, covered with butter and seasoning salt, in one of those gigantic silver bowls. We would get a box of Kleenex for Mom, especially if the movie was something by Disney. The lights went out and the familiar sound of the movie beginning echoed through the living room. I used to love how Dad would laugh when we were watching comedies and get the whole family laughing, or how Mom would cheer on the underdog, sitting at the edge of her seat, saying, "Go! Go! Go!" I don't know exactly why watching a movie bonded our family the way it did, but it had a very profound effect on me, and I miss those days.

It was a disastrous blow and an indescribable change when we stopped doing all the things we used to as a family. I would say that the loss of our family unit was the most painful aspect of the divorce for me to deal with. The only way I can begin to describe what it was like is to compare it to a death—because that is really what it was …

a death. We needed to acknowledge our loss, mourn, and grieve as though we had lost a loved one.

Divorce had become so common that when it happened to my parents, acknowledging my loss was difficult. I felt like I shouldn't be hurt or angry, because everyone was doing it. What was the big deal? And yet it hurt so badly. I needed to know it was okay to hurt, to be angry, and to grieve. However, divorce doesn't have the same final impact as death. Closure becomes an impossible task. A divorce evolves into a lifelong journey, presenting new circumstances to deal with as you go along.

For a long time, I let the pain linger in my heart by dwelling on what I had lost. Then I decided to cherish the moments that I had had with my family—to remember the great times at the hockey rink, at the lake cabin, on the baseball field, on holiday trips, and at home.

Sometimes we have to accept that life won't always be fair, and appreciate what we do have by making the best of it. Losing my family unit eventually gave me a new appreciation for my own children and the family that I have created. I now have the chance to bring those moments I cherished back into my life with my own kids.

The First Christmas

Christmas is my favorite time of year; it always has been. I love celebrating with the family, feeling the Christmas spirit in the air, watching snowflakes gently fall to the ground, devouring a Christmas feast, enjoying friendly conversation with strangers, hearing the sounds of Christmas carols echoing in the wind, seeing bright Christmas lights shining from house to house, and feeling the joy of sharing gifts with my loved ones. I love Christmas.

However, Christmas, and all of our family gatherings, changed drastically after my parents divorced. The family traditions we had formed through the years were altered to accommodate the new situation. Christmas became a very difficult and frustrating time of year for me. I still love Christmas, but in a different way than I did when my family was together.

As I was growing up, our family followed a Christmas tradition every year. It started with Christmas Eve dinner at my aunt and uncle's on my mom's side. It was the most exciting time. I loved the anticipation leading up to Christmas morning. My grandma and all of my cousins, uncles, and aunts would attend the dinner. We would arrive at around 4:00 PM, and within a half-hour, we kids were down in the basement for a hockey showdown as the parents enjoyed an abundance of hors d'oeuvres. Our cousins, Wes, and I would each get ten shots on goal, and whoever scored the most would triumph in victory at suppertime! My dad was always a big part of entertaining my cousins at the hockey showdown, typically sharing goalie duties with my uncle. The showdown became a fierce competition between us cousins, and every year like clockwork, one of us would end up getting hurt, ending the hockey ritual. But we loved it!

Christmas dinner would follow, and it was always a feast: roast, chicken, sometimes turkey, mashed potatoes, baked potatoes with sour cream and chives, corn, peas, salads, gravy, mushrooms, and of course, desserts to follow. Every year, I would indulge and stuff myself silly! After dinner, the whole family would sit in the living room and visit, waiting for our food to digest and anxiously anticipating the time to open gifts. Soon, my cousins and I would become too rambunctious, so my aunts would start passing the gifts out, one to each person. On Mom's side of the family, we always chose names at Thanksgiving for the Christmas Eve gift exchange. Then mysteriously, Santa Claus would make a guest appearance and bring gifts for all the little ones. After the gifts were opened and Santa made his debut, one of my uncles would pull out his guitar and lead the family in singing Christmas carols. That was my dad's cue to perform and the cue for us cousins to head for the basement and quickly find something else to do!

Shortly after 11:00 PM, Mom, Dad, Wes, and I would leave for midnight Mass. As the priest conducted his sermon, we sat patiently, eagerly anticipating the best part of Christmas Eve. My parents always allowed us to open a gift from under the tree before we went to bed. The sound of Christmas music played softly in the background: "Silent night, holy night, all is calm, all is bright...." The Christmas-tree lights blinked on and off as Dad, Wes, and I sat around the tree, deciding what gift to open, while Mom made us hot chocolate with little marshmallows. It was a peaceful feeling. We would laugh, joke, sing, and share a loving moment as a family. I loved it.

Christmas morning would come, usually at about 6:30 AM. Mom would play some Christmas music as we opened all the gifts under the tree. Without missing a beat, every year after the gifts were opened, my dad took it upon himself to slip in some Johnny Horton or Buddy Holly on the stereo. Dad's all-time favorites—"The Battle of New Orleans," "Rave On," or "Oh, Boy!"—would belt out of the speakers as he, Wes, and I sang along. Christmas morning was always a blast! My mom and dad made breakfast (not pancakes) and took pictures as Wes and I played our annual Christmas handball hockey game in the living room. At about one o'clock, we would head to my grandma's house on my dad's side for another turkey lunch and Christmas ritual. We would visit with our other cousins, uncles, and aunts, exchange gifts, and again I would overindulge myself silly with turkey, stuffing, mashed potatoes with gravy, three kinds of pie, and one of my favorites, my grandma's twenty-four-hour salad. Christmas was a special time for my family.

The first Christmas after the divorce was the hardest. My dad's sense of humor, spirit, and presence were missing on Christmas Eve, and it was equally hard not having Mom there on Christmas Day. Wes and I missed the comfort and joy we used to share as a family. I felt that I had lost a part of Christmas; I think everyone did. Although we carried out the same traditions, there was a huge piece missing, a piece we would never have again.

Christmas Eve had a different atmosphere. There was a feeling of loss, I believe, throughout the family. It was much more quiet and refined. People were soft-spoken and no one said too much to me. I didn't know what to say to anyone else, either. My dad wasn't there for the first time. I hoped other people would open the conversations. I think they felt the same way about me, because I ended up keeping to myself and not much was said. I missed my dad terribly. He wasn't there to entertain my cousins as he did every year—wrestling, laughing, playing hockey, or just joking around. He wasn't there to hand out the Christmas song sheets and take lead vocals as the parents sang "The Twelve Days of Christmas," or to help clean up the leftovers after everyone was done eating a third or fourth helping. And he wasn't there to be in our annual family picture.

I didn't want anyone to know how much it hurt to not have my dad there, but at the same time, I was getting mad that no one was acknowledging him. At first, no one said anything about Dad—as if he hadn't been there for the past seventeen years. As the night progressed, it was hard to dismiss the feeling that no one cared that he was missing. It was a pretty awkward situation and I'm sure they didn't want to upset Mom, Wes, or me. However, it really hurt that after all the years Dad spent being a part of the Christmas Eve celebration, it felt like he was forgotten. It was exactly the same way on Christmas Day at my grandma's house; it was as though Mom no longer existed.

It wasn't until we were leaving that first Christmas Eve that one of my aunts came over and presented me with a gift, neatly wrapped inside a paper bag, to pass on to my dad. She handed me the gift, politely asking me to give it to him. Surprised, I looked up at her in appreciation. Tears built up in our eyes as she quickly told me that my dad would be missed, and I thanked her for the gift. It was the only time that happened over the years, but I will never forget it as long as I live. My aunt will never know how much that meant to me—knowing that somewhere underneath it all, they did care.

It's unfortunate that each parent has to become removed from the other side of the family. After a divorce, though, the truth is that ultimately, they are no longer part of each other's family—even though their children always will be.

Shock Waves Ripple Through the Family

The announcement of my parents' breakup not only shocked me, but it sent shock waves rippling throughout the family. Surprise and confusion were the shared sentiments. My parents' separation caught family members off-guard, leaving them somewhat dumb-founded. After all, they had been married for seventeen years and dated for five years as high-school sweethearts. My parents had a history, a lifetime together with two children. They had made it through good and bad times and were the "happy" couple, except behind closed doors.

The reactions of extended family members varied across the board. They included everything from absolute shock to angry confrontations, and comments ranged from, "What on earth are you doing?" to "It's none of our business; we won't get involved." Everyone had his or her own way of dealing with it. What I found amazing and difficult to deal with was the fact that the people who I thought wouldn't say anything bad, and would try to help the situation, ended up being the ones who flew off the handle. The people I thought would talk to my parents and straighten the mess out—the ones I was secretly counting on to come out of the woodwork and say all the right things—decided to stay out of it, because they felt it was none of their business. Each reaction brought unique challenges and stirred up tender emotions in me.

One of the items on my wish list for family members was that they didn't take sides. I loved both Mom and Dad, and I wanted everyone else to do the same. I didn't want anyone hating my mom or my dad because of the divorce. However, that just wasn't in the cards for everyone.

Thinking back to the different things that happened between the families because of the divorce, I am reminded of many crazy occurrences that even today continue to develop and sometimes erupt. I don't know everything that was said and done, and that's probably good. Nevertheless, going through a divorce means you need to expect the unexpected. Without divulging all of the dirt, many interesting things happened within my family circle—like hiring a private investigator to help eliminate the possibility of an affair, or feuding between family members about why my parents divorced or what could have been done to prevent it. Wild accusations were made, secrets were revealed, and I was left holding the bag, fishing through anger, pain, reality, fear, and stories in an attempt to find the truth.

Despite some of the craziness, however, both sides of my family were there for my parents, Wes, and me when we needed it. They would help us whenever they could. We could have never made it through without their support, kindness, and help!

My parents' divorce was like a pebble being dropped in water. It rippled out, touching, hurting, and sometimes causing unforgivable pain in our family members' lives. Divorce impacts so many people and it reflects on the whole family, whether or not they are directly involved. It changes people's lives forever.

Today, I am still faced with times that are not easy to deal with amongst family members, and sometimes I find myself getting to a point where I just don't want to listen to anymore talk. I find that the best thing for me to do if discussions become difficult is assert some ground rules, like avoiding ridiculing or directly bashing my mom or dad when we talk. It works better. I have learned to always be true to myself no matter what others think. I find we need to question others' opinions and decide for ourselves what we believe by searching for the truth.

What's Happening to Me?

As time went on, not only did my emotions run wild with all the changes that the divorce brought, but my state of mind began to change, too. I didn't know what was happening to me. I became depressed and serious. Little things that bothered me were magnified into huge ordeals, and I really didn't like who I was anymore. With all of the changes, I felt like my life was going wrong in so many directions. I just wanted to give up. Somehow, my life just wasn't as important to me as it once was. It's confusing enough just to be a teenager. As my emotions about various aspects of my life—both related and not related to the divorce—got tangled together, I was on my way to becoming a nervous wreck. I didn't care as much about hockey, my family, and especially school—which wasn't good, because it wasn't like I was a straight-A student. In addition, I gradually started to feel like I was losing some of my friends.

It became difficult talking with friends because I was so depressed about my parents' divorce. My mind was always somewhere else. I couldn't get as excited about activities I normally would have, and I couldn't have fun like I used to. The truth was that I was frantically looking for someone to lean on. I was about to break down, but I didn't want anyone to know I was hurting. I was a popular student in high school, where a person's reputation is an important commodity. I didn't want people thinking that I cried, needed help, or was upset. I didn't know that I could ask for support or talk to others about the situation. I wanted someone to wave a magic wand and make everything better.

I had changed, and not for the better. For a time, I was ignored. My friends didn't confide in me or include me like they normally had. I couldn't seem to connect with anyone. Feeling like I had lost my friends, I didn't realize that what really happened was that my friends lost me. I wasn't the same person after my parents divorced. I was angry at the world, and the reason I felt alone was that I kept pushing everyone away.

There was one particular time in high school when I exploded. I really over-reacted because of how the divorce was affecting me. That was the day I realized I needed to start talking about it and not keep my feelings inside.

It was a Friday afternoon, the end of the school week. One of my close friends, Tim, was hosting a party that night. I knew that many of my friends were going. For some reason, the whole day had gone by and I still had not been invited. It didn't make sense. Since it was just a high-school party, perhaps I didn't need an invite. But this was Tim, a long-time good friend, and he would always tell me about a party he was hosting. All I could think was that he didn't want me there.

By the time the school bell rang at the end of the day, I was furious. I slammed my books into my locker and was preparing to head straight home, when I saw Tim and some of our friends huddled by the front door. I assumed they were all secretly talking about the party. The closer I got to them, the more they whispered, which only affirmed my suspicions. I was sure they were whispering about me not being invited to the party. I plotted my revenge tactic: I would just walk right on by and not say a word. The silent treatment is the best defense.

I was almost out the front doors when Tim shouted, "Craig, I'm having a party tonight. I'll pick you up later, okay?" I couldn't believe it. Tim had had plenty of time to invite me, but he waited until now. I figured it must be out of sheer guilt. If that was the case, I didn't want him doing me any favors! I stopped and turned towards the group, ready to give them all a piece of my mind, when Tim walked over to me and asked, "What time can I pick you up at?" I paused as the tension in my body mounted. I told him, "No thanks, Tim. I'm not going." He gave me a puzzled look and said, "Come on, I will pick you up. It will be a blast."

As Tim was giving me the party sales pitch, I heard Bridget's voice in the background: "Craig's parents split up?" It was an innocent comment that I took as an attack. I felt like the gossip about my parents suggested my family wasn't as good as others—somehow making me less of a person. It just hit me, confirming the reason I thought I hadn't been invited to the party earlier. I exploded, yelling at the top of my lungs, "Yes, my parents are split up! Is it any of your damn business, Bridget?" I was so embarrassed that my parents were divorced. I turned to Tim and told him he could stuff his party! My friends stared at me in amazement. I probably could have passed for the PA system; I had shouted so loudly. I was ready to burst so I rushed out the front doors and began running home.

I never did go to the party, but the following week, I found out the real reason why I wasn't invited right away. The party was supposed to be a surprise intended to cheer me up, but I had found out about it. I didn't know what to say. I felt like Fred Flintstone in the episode where Fred put his foot in his mouth and got to wear the "First-Class Heel" award tattooed to his forehead.

That was the day I realized what a jerk I had been to some of my friends. After the divorce, everything changed. I didn't know how to open up or talk about the things that were happening to me. I was embarrassed and on uncharted waters. I never realized that my friends were going through a similar experience, not knowing what to do or say to me about it. I went for a long time believing no one cared and feeling that I didn't belong anymore. I felt like less of a person than my friends. Instead of dealing with how I felt, I resented my friends for it, even though they did nothing wrong. Isn't that nuts?

As I journeyed along, I found true friends. Interestingly, my relationships with many of my friends changed. Some friendships grew stronger, and some were lost altogether because they turned out not to be true friends. I also formed new friendships with people I hadn't known very well before my parents' divorce, but now could strongly relate to. We're left vulnerable in a crisis, and we find our true friends in the people who care about us. They care to lend a shoulder and just listen without judgment.

Living Out of a Suitcase

Eventually, I did go live with my mom. Over time, my dad got a new job which required him to be out of town for weeks at a time, forcing me to go back and forth from Mom's to Dad's depending on his work schedule. Being caught in the middle of my parents' various moves to different houses, and then having to go back and forth between them, was exhausting. It also made it extremely hard to gain any stability or security in my life. It felt like I was living out of my suitcase, constantly packing. I was staying in one place just long enough to feel settled, and then it would be time to pack up again.

Frustrated, I longed to be able to call one place my home—to have that "home sweet home" feeling. I wanted to have a connection to a place where I felt like I belonged. I couldn't have just one home, so after time, I found the next best thing was to put a piece of myself in the house I was staying in.

When I first started staying at Mom's, I couldn't sleep in my room. I had to sleep on the living room floor in front of the television. At the time, I couldn't understand why I did that, and it drove my mom nuts. For the longest time after Mom left the family home, I spent almost every night on the floor in front of the TV. I would put a blanket on the carpet and cuddle up in my sleeping bag, letting the sound of the television help me fall asleep. I hated the silence in my bedroom. When my parents were married, we were always hosting company at our house and it was a very busy household. I grew accustomed to sleeping regardless of the noise, as it was comfortable and familiar to me. The silence would flood anxiety through my body, allowing me too much time to think. I felt lonely and overwhelmed. I needed a release at the end of the day, and that became the television.

It took me almost two years, and countless attempts by my parents to get me to sleep in my room, before I found a new release in working out with weights at the gym. Working out was great for releasing stress, not to mention for getting in remarkable shape. I could take my anger out on the weights, which left me exhausted, ready for bed, and less dependent on the television. Still, I put my stereo beside my bed and listened to music at night. I just didn't like silence.

After moving in full-time with Mom, I felt I needed to find a way to make her home feel like it was mine too. Up until then, it had felt more like a hotel. I needed to be a part of it, to have my own space and have something that would symbolize that I belonged.

I got an idea! There was a half-finished rumpus room in Mom's basement. I had some friends over, and we were joking around and having fun down downstairs when I unleashed my plan. I wanted to convert the rumpus room into a real party room—with a stereo system, some couches, a table and chairs, and a bar in the corner. My friends embraced the idea and we instantly held a brainstorming session on how we could construct a private bar and party room. This would give me my own space, put a part of me in the house, and allow me to bond with my friends, which was a big priority for me at the time. I had a winning plan with only one major obstacle: Mom.

After a few hours, my friends and I had our blueprints ready. All we needed to do was purchase the materials and get to work. I knew my mom wouldn't like this idea. However, I also knew that she almost never went into the rumpus room downstairs. That meant it was conceivable that I didn't have to ask or tell her at all. Why ruin a good plan, right? That turned out to be a mistake a little later on! Nevertheless, I was determined. I pulled some money out of my savings and waited until the weekend to start the project, as I knew Mom would be out on a date one night.

My friends came over and we all went to work building our private bar. It was fun—fun I had been longing for. We felt accomplished after the framework was done. It looked awesome. It stood almost four feet tall and five feet wide, with two posts on each side to hold up the sign that ran across the top: "The Bar." Instead of painting it, I decided to cover it with a collage of beer labels. I was working at a restaurant at the time, so I had access to tons of empty beer bottles. After closing time, I would quickly run the empties through the dishwasher to heat them up, which allowed me to peel off perfect labels. My co-workers thought I was nuts, but I had great ambition. It took over five hundred labels, plastered to the top and the sides of the bar, to complete the collage. I left some space available at the front so that everyone who came over when Mom was out could sign his or her name as a tribute to partying at "The Bar!"

Partying at the bar became a tradition amongst my friends, but more importantly, it gave me a feeling of belonging in the home.

Lessons in Change

There is a universal rule that I learned from my experience: the only thing in life that remains constant is change. Change is something many of us fear and do not like. Change can be difficult to deal with and can cause our lives to go entirely out of balance. There were so many changes in my life after my parents split up that I didn't have enough time to even think about one change before another one took its place. The life that I had known was flipped upside down and inside out. From all of these changes came many great life lessons, most of which took time to learn. Actually, they took years to learn, and I am still learning more every day. It feels like I have been cursed to be someone who always has to learn by his mistakes.

I have discovered that change can be bad or good. Life is all about change. It is what we do with the changes in our lives that counts. We can learn lessons that will help us get to where we want to go in life, or we can run from change because it is too difficult to deal with and accept. I think that for the most part, we often run away from change when it strikes because it can be a scary thing. Most people resist it and hate it. I did, because it was so difficult to find security in my life. Getting through the day became my biggest challenge for a period of time. It took me a long time to realize I needed to learn from all the changes—to ask myself, "What's going on here? And how does this affect me? What can I do to cope and to make it better for myself and for others?"

Life will continue to bring changes. It's up to us to ask the questions, examine our hearts, and use the lessons we learn to reshape the outcome and result. How do we begin to control the changes in our lives? I heard an anonymous statement a long time ago that answers that question, and I believe it defines what it means to learn from the lessons change provides: "The best way to predict the future is to create it!"

The Most Important Thing is the Truth

There is much wisdom in the old cliché that "the truth will set you free." For me, needing to know the truth about why my parents split up became an obsession. The more I couldn't get an answer or the answer didn't make sense, the harder I would push. I didn't care what it was or how bad the reason; I wanted to know the truth about why Mom and Dad had to get divorced.

As rumors and speculation surfaced, all kinds of wild ideas came out. Affairs, bad influences, misunderstandings, secrets from the past, unresolved issues—all of these were claimed to be the cause of the divorce. I found myself getting caught up in it. Who did this? Who did that? I felt like a yo-yo, and it was getting me nowhere and ripping me apart.

When the accusations finally became too much, I confronted Mom again. It must have been two years since my parents had split up when I asked her, "Mom, why did you really leave?" She said many things in answer to my question, but one thing really got inside of me. Mom said, "When I left your dad, one of the most important things to me was to have you and Wes live your lives in truth. When I thought about how my leaving would affect you and your brother, I concluded that it was far more important for you boys to know the truth and live in what's real, rather than to continue to learn the destructive patterns and phoniness your dad and I had developed over the years."

Once I decided not to look for one main reason why, but to instead try and put myself in my parents' shoes and realize why they felt the way they did, I understood better. I then became free of my obsessive need to know why. Sometimes there are no concrete answers, just bits and pieces of reasoning. For instance, when I asked myself what had happened to make my parents grow apart, I started piecing little parts of the puzzle together. Mom felt like she had lost her identity. Her true feelings were never being heard and acknowledged. Dad felt like Mom didn't support his ideas and ambitions. My parents worked in conflicting environments. Financial stress ate away at their relationship because disagreements about money led to resentment. My parents began to slip away from each other as they created different agendas and moved towards separate goals in life. They didn't work as a team like they once had. They wanted different things. Their beliefs about life became different. And in the midst of it all, they never stopped to reconnect with each other and move closer together. Instead, the patterns they had created left them shackled, consistently pushing each other further away, and they grew apart over time.

During the discussion with my mom, I realized I needed to look beyond the surface, because the truth doesn't lie in the countless rumors and speculation. It lies deep within, where we are most vulnerable and we can't hide from what's real.

I realized in the end that I wanted to know more than just why my parents divorced. I wanted to know the truth about myself. I wanted to know the truth about who I was now, where I belonged, what my family was, and if and why I was loved. Finding the truth to those questions became the most important thing—allowing me to focus on my life and myself.

CHAPTER THREE

Identity Crisis

"Life is full of choices and challenges. It's how you adapt to them that will determine your future."

~Jeff Ivanochko

I had a provincial playoff hockey game—game five in a best-of-five series. I was waiting for Dad to pick me up and take me to the arena. Over my hockey years, my parents came out to most of the games and supported my dream to become a professional hockey player. They wanted me to play in the NHL, and I think there were times when they felt that someday I would. However, after the breakup, it all seemed to change. My parents had become wrapped up in their own problems and didn't have the time to come and watch or even drive me to hockey. Wes and I kind of got lost in the mix for a while, in the heat of the turmoil. Other things became more important to my parents, and I didn't know what to make of it. Their actions led me to believe that they had lost faith in me—that they didn't support me anymore. I started to doubt whether they ever really believed that I would make my dream come true and make the NHL. Dad wasn't expressing how proud he was of me like he used to, and Mom never seemed to have time to talk hockey like we once did. They both became less interested as time went on. Hockey was becoming a problem, time-wise and money-wise, and I was starting to think they wanted me to quit. That's when I stopped believing in myself.

It was getting late, and if Dad didn't pick me up soon, I wasn't going to get to my hockey game on time. I was getting very impatient. He was always running behind in those days. He said it was because of the huge demands put on him at work, but if you ask me, it was because he had verbal diarrhea everywhere he went. Once he got talking, he would talk forever! Finally, I saw his car pull up in the driveway and we were off. He apologized for being late and seemed to be quite frustrated with all the running around he had been doing lately. As we drove to the arena, he mentioned that we should maybe look into getting a car for me so I could drive myself to hockey games. Although I was disappointed that he was possibly suggesting he wouldn't be coming to my games anymore, that was overruled by the excitement I felt about getting a car!

With extreme zeal, I helped Dad rationalize the idea of getting me a car by expressing my deep concern about needing to drive to hockey. I also stressed the other things I could help out with—like taking care of errands or driving Wes to his hockey games. In the back of my mind, though, I knew I needed the car for one colossal purpose: impressing girls! I managed to convince my dad that I should have a car. The catch was that I would have to use some of my own money, because times were tight. I felt that the five hundred dollars I had saved up would be enough, so I told Dad it was a great idea.

All the way to the hockey arena, we talked about purchasing a car. Most of the discussion was Dad lecturing me about how big of a responsibility it was to own a car, as I nodded my head in agreement to all of his critical points.

Finally, very late, we arrived at the arena. Dad stopped the car in front of the doors, and in a rush, I grabbed my gear and ran to the dressing room. As I passed through the lobby, I quickly looked to see if my mom was in the stands. She had said she would be there, and I was hoping she could make it because she had missed the previous four games. Tonight's was an important one—we were playing the final, tie-breaking game to advance in the provincials. I didn't see Mom sitting anywhere, though. I had just enough time to get dressed, endure a heated lecture from the coach about being late, and get on the ice for the opening face-off.

By the middle of the second period, my team was winning. I could see Dad standing at the end of the rink, watching attentively, but I still couldn't see Mom. I was sitting on the bench, feeling disappointed that she wasn't there. She had promised. I took a second look at the usual places she would be sitting, and still couldn't see her. Then, out of the corner of my eye, I caught sight of her standing alone by the glass on the opposite side of the arena. I was really glad she had come, but I felt a sense of pain when I saw her standing there by herself. The coached yelled, "Craig, your line's up. Get moving!" I skated out to the center of the ice. I could see both of my parents at opposite ends of the rink, by themselves, with intense, serious expressions on their faces. And then there was me—right smack in the middle. It suddenly became painfully clear to me that my family was divided! The play continued in the game, but I couldn't get into it. I kept fighting back my tears, hoping no one would notice how fragile I was at that moment.

I felt like Mom and Dad had divided into two teams, and I was the referee—trying to bring order, reason, structure, and rules into their chaotic game of divorce. That moment became symbolic to me, and the vision of that night still lingers in my mind. My dad was on one side and my mom on the other. Where did I fit in? I was caught in the middle. It was the beginning of my identity crisis, my search to find where I truly belonged in the family. My team ended up winning that game and my teammates were elated because we were moving on to the next round of the provincials. But to me, it felt like a loss. I had lost my spirit.

Who was I if we didn't have a family anymore? How could I be a part of something if it didn't exist? What was I a part of? Would I always feel caught in the middle? Did it mean I was a failure because my family failed? On the way home that night, I didn't say much. Dad tried to cheer me up by talking about how exciting it would be to get me a car. It worked a bit, but I couldn't shake my confusion.

Am I a Failure?

Car shopping took my mind off of my problems for awhile. I purchased a used-car magazine and began flipping through the pages, circling all of the cars that were under a thousand dollars but still looked better than old relics. I had five hundred dollars saved, and I figured I could probably borrow a little bit from my parents if I had to. After shopping around a little, I realized I couldn't find a car with tires for five hundred dollars!

I had looked at about five or six lemons when I came across my car. It was a 1977 bright-orange Ventura. It looked similar to the General Lee from the "Dukes of Hazzard" television show. It was the car I wanted! The asking price was seven hundred dollars, and the car was in fair condition. It was definitely the best car I had seen up to that point. I was so excited—my first car!

However, I had two problems. I didn't have my license yet, because I was a couple months shy of being sixteen and couldn't yet drive legally. In addition, I was short two hundred dollars. After pleading with my dad, I was able to talk him into letting me buy the car by suggesting that if we didn't buy it right away, someone else would in short order. He agreed and made me promise to let it sit in the driveway until I passed my driver's test. I promised, and then began plotting how to ask my parents for two hundred dollars. I gave them the best sales pitch I could come up with, sugar-coating it by telling them how responsible I would be. With a little brown-nosing, I was able to get them to agree to lend me a hundred dollars each so that I could purchase the car. I was in business, and now had what I thought would be the ultimate babe-magnet. Well, I guess that truthfully, I was still going to have to rely on my charm. On pins and needles with excitement, I helped Dad write up the deal and the car was mine. I just had to get it home. Since I didn't have a license, I asked my friend Will to come with me to pick up the car and drive it home.

The car was neatly washed and shining brightly in the sun when Dad, Will, and I arrived to pick it up. I remember climbing in and sitting behind the wheel for the first time as the owner. I felt the spirit of freedom at my fingertips, picturing the wind blowing through my hair and beautiful girls lounging throughout the car. I looked at Will, he looked at me, and we both smiled. I moved over to the co-pilot's seat as Will started the car and revved the engine. The car had an old tape deck in the dash, so I had brought a cassette with a special song to christen my bright-orange party machine! I placed the cassette in the deck and turned the volume up full-blast. Will and I waited for the song, Kenny Loggins' "Welcome to Heartlight," to belt out of the speakers. Then Will floored the gas pedal, spun the tires in a screeching roar, and we headed out into the world, feeling independent and free.

Like I had promised my dad, I parked the car in the driveway. I sat in it every day, waiting for my birthday. The car became a sanctuary for me. I would listen to music and think for hours. Music provided a release for me, soothing the pain I felt as a result of all of the other things going on in my life at the time.

My birthday finally came and I scheduled my driver's examination for a Monday morning. Dad drove me to my test and waited in the office, as I had decided to use his car for the exam since it was compact and easier to parallel park. I'm sure he was thinking, "Please God, let Craig bring the car back in one piece!" The instructor sat in the passenger's seat of the car. We buckled up our seatbelts and the instructor told me to back up, make a right turn, and flow into traffic. I was pumped! This was going to be a piece of cake! Up until that point, I had only driven around town with Dad a handful of times. However, with my enthusiasm, I felt ready to race in the Indy 500.

As I made the right turn, flowing into traffic, I noticed a clipboard on the instructor's lap. He had written three number tens beside different point categories. I felt good so far—I had gotten ten out of ten on three different things! What I didn't know was that those numbers were actually demerit points, and if I got over fifty, I would fail. I kept driving, occasionally glancing over at the instructor's clipboard. He had put two more tens on the sheet. I was getting excited! Ten out of ten! Oh ya! I was thinking to myself, "I'm good. I'm really, really good," as I figured I was acing the test. I had almost finished the exam when I got caught in the middle of an intersection waiting to make a left-hand turn, because someone ran a red light coming towards me in the opposite lane. I couldn't tell if the instructor was upset with the guy who ran the red light or with me, because he was shaking his head and mumbling to himself as I quickly proceeded out of the intersection. However, he put two more tens on my sheet, so I concluded that I must have handled the situation right. Soon after, I parallel-parked the car, and that completed my exam. Again, I glanced at the instructor's sheet and noticed a total of seven scores of ten! I was feeling alive and more than ready to get my picture taken for my driver's license! The instructor was giving me the standard lecture, explaining which things I did well and which I did poorly. I was anxiously waiting for him to get to the part where he would say, "Let's go inside and take your picture," when he said, "Craig, I have tallied your score and I will need you to take a driver's training course before you come back to take the test over." I questioned him, "Over? Didn't I pass?" He told me that, unfortunately, I had failed. Shocked, I said, "What? I failed? But I saw your sheet! I scored ten out of ten on almost everything!" He roared in laughter as he explained, "Those tens are demerit points and if you get over fifty points, you fail. You scored seventy points."

I failed my driver's test. I was crushed! Completely embarrassed, I felt immense emotions rise up inside of me, just like the lava in a volcano—emotions I had been avoiding and bottling up for a long time because of my excitement about getting my license. Out of nowhere, I could feel an eruption ready to blow. I didn't mean to, but I started shouting at the instructor, "Get out! Get out now! Take your demerit points and…!" Stunned, he got out of the car. Leaving the instructor standing there, I slammed the transmission into drive and sped across the parking lot, where Dad was waiting for me. He climbed into the car and asked me, with great concern, "Craig, what's going on?" I said abruptly, "I failed!" and proceeded to drive home. Dad didn't say much on the way home. He just continually glanced my way, about to speak, and then turned away. It was the first time in a long time that I had seen such disappointment in his eyes.

I failed. It was a part of life, but a tough one to take. It hit me like a piercing arrow, because I decided that I didn't just fail my test, but that I was a failure. I had always felt successful in the eyes of my parents—as a hockey player, an athlete, a friend, a son, and even a student. But now, in the last year, it was like it didn't matter how hard I tried; I couldn't do anything right! What was I now? Someone who couldn't even pass a simple driving test. I went from a future NHL prospect to a complete failure.

Failing my driver's exam acted as a trigger point of many events that left me feeling like a failure because it seemed that suddenly everything I had been good at, I wasn't anymore. I lost my confidence, my belief in myself, as so many things in my life changed rapidly because of the divorce. I was so overwhelmed that little hurts and pains along the way—like failing my driver's test—became absolute tragedies for me. It was as though the pain from the divorce automatically magnified anytime something didn't work out for me, pushing me farther down into self-destruction. Was I really a failure? No. I failed my driver's test because I hadn't learned how to drive properly. It didn't mean I was a complete failure. It meant I needed driver's training. After I got expert instruction, I realized how much I needed to learn, and I passed the second test with flying colors.

It was the same with my parents' divorce. I wasn't a failure because my parents' marriage didn't work. It had nothing to do with me. It took me a long time to learn that I was my own person, and that my failures as well as my successes were going to be mine alone—just like my parents' were.

Unfortunately, as with my failed driver's test, I needed to learn more life lessons to prepare me for the new and fast-paced challenges coming my way. I was sent spinning into a whirlwind of insecurity, constantly questioning my future.

Was My Life a Lie?

One night I couldn't sleep. I lay in bed, staring at the ceiling and listening to the radio. As I listened, I found myself beginning to panic.

I had reached an ultimate low in my identity crisis, and I was entangled in emotions. One question continually rang out in my mind: Was my whole life nothing but one gigantic lie? I was feeling completely lost and insecure, not knowing where I belonged in the world. I had committed myself to a belief that I had become a complete failure, so the answer, "Yes, it was a lie," felt so real. My life had become so different from what it used to be. I felt like my parents had been putting on an act in their marriage, and their life together had been nothing but a lie—up until the divorce, when the truth started to emerge. Because their marriage felt like a lie, and I was part of that, I felt like my life must have been a lie too.

I began to question whether all of our loving memories and good times together had been real. I wondered if my parents had been pretending. I began to wonder why I was even born, and whether or not my parents had really wanted me as their son. I wanted to know that I was born out of love. I wanted to know that I was important in their lives. I began doubting my parents' love for me because they didn't love each other. That made me think that loving me was probably a lie, too. That thought was too much for me. I became filled with rage as I wrapped my head in my pillow, desperately needing to know that my parents loved me.

For the next few weeks, I became very withdrawn and depressed. I walked around in a stupor, jealous of friends and people who belonged to loving families. I felt like I was somehow less worthy than they were. I wanted so badly to have my family together, but there was just no hope.

Focusing on avoiding my pain became too much to handle. I couldn't avoid it any longer. It was attacking me so strongly. I needed to know—to be certain if my life was a lie, if I was born out of love, if I was wanted, if I was loved! I felt so stupid for thinking all of those things that it was absolutely the most difficult and awkward thing for me to ask about—but deep down, I had to know either way. I couldn't take it. I had to confront my fear, no matter how stupid it seemed. Finally, I dug down deep, despite being mortified about how I felt, and after about twenty failed attempts, I built up the courage to ask my mom. Before Mom had time to put her book down, I put it all on the line and unloaded: "Mom, has my life been a lie? Do you and Dad still love me? Were you and Dad ever in love? Are all the good memories I have of our family fake or pretend too? Was I even born out of love? Was I meant to be? Did you and Dad really want me?"

Mom's face dropped in horror; she was astonished that I would ask such questions. She assured me over and over that I was very much wanted—that she loved me very much, as did my dad, and that just because they were divorced, it didn't mean they never loved each other or that the memories weren't real. It felt good to hear her say that, and it was a big relief for me to get it off my chest, even though part of me felt ridiculous and silly. I needed clarification and reassurance from my mom in order to put my heart at ease and bury my doubt.

Seeking Out Counseling

As time went on, I was starting to feel better. I wasn't as scared, knowing that my parents still loved me. I thought I was handling the situation and accepting more and more things as time went on. I was still struggling, but I was surviving! I was having bad days and good days regarding my parents' situation. I was trying hard to take one thing at a time and slow things down to where I could actually deal with them. I felt like I was finally getting a grip and doing pretty well.

My mom had another idea altogether about how I was doing. She wanted me to go to a counselor! She kept encouraging me, explaining that even if I felt okay, it would be good for me to talk to someone objective, to get things off my chest. That really infuriated me! I didn't feel like there was anything wrong with me, and now all of a sudden Mom was telling me there was. At least, that's what I thought. Her intentions were good. All she wanted me to do was let out my emotions and have the opportunity to talk to someone who could help me sort through my feelings. She felt I might be uncomfortable talking to her or Dad, and that it would be easier for me to talk to a counselor. I took it as an attack and was absolutely insulted. I was doing the best I could, and I thought, *How dare my mom insinuate that I need help?* I strongly refused to go, at first. She would ask me every month, and she even phoned the school counselor's office so that they could try to intervene.

I would insist, "I don't need a counselor! I can handle it on my own!" Mom never forced me to go, but she also wouldn't stop mentioning it. Then Dad started suggesting it would be a good idea. Now it was two against one! I felt badly enough about myself. I really didn't need some so-called 'professional' shrink telling me all the things that were wrong with me. I was so mad! I thought to myself that I didn't create all this crap, so why should I need to justify myself in order to prove I was okay? I was trying to do my best to deal with it, and I didn't want to feel like I couldn't. I didn't want to feel like I needed help. I had my pride and my dignity to salvage. The counselor was a threat—the enemy. If anyone found out I was in therapy, I would be a laughingstock.

Finally, I'd had enough of my parents pestering me, so I gave up. I told Mom I would go, but insisted I wasn't going to stay long and there was no way I was going to the school counselor. There was too great a chance of embarrassment if anyone in the school saw me going into the counselor's office. The whole visit was to be strictly top-secret and confidential or I wasn't going. My reputation was at stake and it was too important to risk anyone thinking even less of me.

I can't believe how wrong I was. Looking back on how I felt about certain things, I really have to laugh at myself. Teen years sure are confusing! However, being a teenager is also a time when you learn major lessons about life and yourself.

My mom booked an appointment for me with a counselor in the city. His office was downtown on the top floor of a high-rise, really classy and plush with an incredible view overlooking the entire city. I was impressed. I remember thinking to myself, *My God, people must have problems, because this guy's obviously raking in the dough!* I sat in the waiting room, debating whether or not I should make a break for it. I didn't want to feel like there was something wrong with me. I kept telling myself, "Craig, whatever this counselor might say, there is nothing wrong with you." However, part of the reason I was there was to make sure that there wasn't.

The receptionist called my name: "Craig Leibel." It was my turn. I was nervous and apprehensive about going in. It wasn't exactly how I had envisioned it. There was no padded leather couch or library of books on the wall. When the counselor politely asked me to sit down, I sat in one of the chairs across from his desk.

The counselor began my session by asking me why I was there. All I could tell him was that my parents had divorced a while back, and that they thought it would be best for me to see a counselor to talk about it. He then asked if *I* thought it was best. I didn't know what to say. I was expecting him to tell me that I had a problem and needed to follow a certain set of steps to fix it, but instead he was asking me what my opinion was. That was different. I said, "No, I don't need to see a counselor. I don't think or feel I have a problem and I am doing the best I can to deal with all the changes and difficulties the divorce has created."

He said that was good, and then asked, "Do you know why people come to see a counselor?" I told him, "To fix problems, problems they are experiencing in their lives." He said that might be true to some degree, but that most people come to see a counselor to talk and to find clarity about their feelings. They come to express painful emotions without fear of judgment. They hope to better understand themselves and gain some guidance. I said, "So, the goal is to more or less organize your emotions in order to understand why you feel the way you do, and then use that information to make better choices in your life." He said, "Yes, that's it," and then asked me if I would like to tell him more about how I had been feeling and what I had done to cope with the divorce. I thought, *Wow, I didn't expect it to be like this.* He was giving me a choice, saying it was up to me if I wanted to continue. I said okay, but I wasn't sure how to begin. With encouragement, he told me to take my time and start at the beginning—or that I could say nothing at all, and he would simply ask me questions. I replied that I would rather talk.

I started by telling him how I was shocked about my parents' divorce, angry about the three-month trial idea, and upset that I didn't know the truth. I told him I had been feeling confused as to where I belonged and who I was. I talked about all the new changes and events that had happened, how I felt, and what I did to keep sane. I blasted out stuff for almost an hour, talking about everything I could think of. It felt good.

After we were finished talking, the counselor asked me some intriguing questions. He wanted to know why I felt like I had a problem when I came into his office. I replied that it was because my parents were divorced. He looked at me and said, "That doesn't mean there is anything wrong with you, does it?" I said, "You're right; it doesn't!" He then paused, looked me in the eyes inquisitively, and asked, "Who do you think you're more like—your mom or dad?" I thought this might be some of that reverse psychology stuff, or at least some form of trickery. I collected my thoughts for a moment, looked back at him, and asked, "Why would you want to know that?" He said, "No reason; I am just curious." Peering out at the spectacular view of the city, I thought for a minute about the different characteristics of my mom and dad. I turned toward the counselor and said, "I'm not more like either of them. I'm right in the middle. I'm me." He seemed quite pleased with my answer and ended our conversation by stating, "Craig, the fault of the divorce lies between your parents, not with you. So know that you are okay. You're dealing with a tough time, but you don't have a problem—just courage." I thanked him, shook his hand, and headed home.

It felt good to go to the counselor. I was happy that I did. I was able to get many hurtful and painful emotions off my chest—things I hadn't realized I had been bottling up for a long time. Also, I found out for sure what I thought I already knew: that I didn't have a problem. Later, I did go see the school counselor a couple of times when I felt things were getting hard and out of control. I did it just to check in with myself. I enjoyed the talks and decided that if other people looked down on me for it, it was their loss.

Dealing With Stereotypes and Labels

Why is it that some people make judgments about you when they hear your parents are divorced? Why do they think less of you, assume things about you, or sometimes tack a label to your name without really knowing your character?

I remember one distinct incident when I felt labeled because of the circumstances the divorce brought. The incident left me searching for reasons why others felt I wasn't as good or didn't have much of a future ahead of me. It took place early one morning at my friend John's house. I had stayed over after a late night out, and I woke up with a splitting headache. I could hear John fighting with his dad out in the living room. The door was only halfway open, allowing me to see out of the bedroom, but John and his dad weren't aware that I had woken up. John was standing in front of his dad with his head down, receiving a lengthy lecture about his inexcusable behavior—partying at a bar while underage, coming home late and completely drunk. John and I had snuck into a bar with some others to toast a mutual friend's birthday. In the spirit of fun and birthday celebration, John and I had really over-indulged in the alcohol—especially John, who took it upon himself to be the "drink master," drinking the last of everyone's drink before we were able to escort him out of the building. I called a cab and we went to John's home, where I had told my dad I would be staying.

John's dad effortlessly threw out punishments in his lecture and was very ticked off. What really put him over the edge was the fact that he had to take John—who looked like something out of a Stephen King novel—to his grandmother's birthday lunch later that day. I groaned, and I was just about to put my head back on the pillow when I heard John's dad say, "…and another thing, John! I don't want you hanging out with Craig anymore; he is a bad influence. You know he has family trouble with his parents being split up. I know they don't have much money. With all the drinking going on, I can see he is headed for trouble, and I don't want you going with him."

My chin hit the floor. I was devastated. Shattered, I fought back the tears as I tried to decide how the heck I was going to get out of the house. I had always gotten along well with John's dad previously. I had actually thought he liked me. I couldn't believe that after all of this time, he could pass me off as some kind of bad influence headed for trouble. John's father's words terrified me as I wondered if everyone felt the same way about me.

For years I carried that incident around with me, believing I wasn't as good as my friends, constantly guarding myself and never trusting anything good anybody said about me. The truth is, divorce can cause inappropriate behavior. The immense changes and pain that it results in can influence and alter our normal behavior a great deal. It's easy to lose your head in a crisis. I know I did at times. But ultimately, our behavior is still our responsibility. I don't believe we should stereotype people based on their situations, defining their character based on a circumstance such as divorce. We can only deal with each individual's behavior to make our conclusions. And it doesn't mean things can't change.

I learned that many people assumed that because my parents divorced, I was likely to become a bad kid—a kid with little hope because of the hurdles that I would have to bear. I cared what other people thought, especially the people I respected. I took their comments and criticism to heart, even if I knew it wasn't true. It was so difficult to feel good about myself when others thought less of me. I started buying into the comments I heard. It became easier than thinking I had good qualities and something to offer to the world. I was lost and desperately searching for someone to tell me I was good enough—that just because I came from a broken home, it had nothing to do with my character, who I was, or what I could become, for that matter! I realized later in my life that all the comments, labels, and opinions were a bunch of bull. *I* was the only person who could determine who or what I was going to be.

Living with a negative label can be very difficult and destructive to one's self-esteem. It was for me. I hated being labeled. I learned to let the pain fuel my motivation to build strength in myself. I became determined to prove I had a future and that I would make something of myself, no matter what anybody thought.

Now that I have become a parent, I can see why people judge, label, and stereotype others. We would do anything to protect our children. It's like we build up these defense mechanisms to ensure we keep our children safe from harm. All you have to do is watch the news one night, and how could you not be paranoid? I never understood the parents' side as strongly as I do now.

Although it's common practice in society to label people for various reasons, I believe there are many kids out there who should be given more of a chance. As human beings, it is hard for us not to stereotype or label. I know I'm guilty of it from time to time. However, I believe that if we take the time to open our hearts to others and find out who they really are instead of slamming the door so quickly, we can judge people by their individual actions and characters, not by their circumstances. Then we can make better judgments.

Life's What You Make It!

Hawaii, here we come! Taking the family on a vacation to Hawaii had always been one of my dad's dreams. It was put off over the years for many reasons: my parents were busy making a living, they had other commitments, Wes and I had hockey, or we just didn't have enough money. But this time was different. We were in the midst of chaos and didn't have anything else to lose. Even though we didn't have the money, my dad, with my grandma's help, was determined to take my brother and me on a trip to Hawaii—to show us the time of our lives, lift our spirits, and live out a dream. Ironically, divorce has its benefits, too!

At first, I couldn't help but wonder if my dad was somehow trying to get back at my mom by springing the Hawaii trip we had talked about taking as a family on us—especially when we couldn't afford it. The satisfaction probably was a big motivator, but later I realized that Dad had a more important reason. Somewhere in his heart, I believe he intended our trip to be about teaching us that life is what you make it. Despite your hardships, failures, mistakes, tough times, or uncontrollable circumstances, from this moment on, the rest of your life is what you make it! That reason became more important than money or getting back at my mom.

It was December 24th, at about six o'clock in the morning. I was standing at the airport terminal with Wes, Dad, and my grandma, ready to board the plane and fly to Hawaii. My brother and I were extremely excited about seeing the massive waves, white-sand beaches, and of course the bikini scenery that came with Hawaii! Aloha! Dad had been preparing us with stories of his bodysurfing feats from his trip to the islands when he was a teenager. He told us that he had stared death in the eyes and conquered six-foot waves, riding them right up to the beach. That was to be our first mission—to head for the enormous waves at the beach and bodysurf, conquering seven-foot waves (one foot higher than Dad) like no one had done before! We were pumped!

Christmas is the busy season for tourists vacationing to the tropical islands of Hawaii, and our plane was jam-packed. I couldn't believe the number of passengers the 747 jumbo jet could accommodate. There were many families with little children, all of them excited about Christmas and Santa Claus. I remember overhearing a little girl at the terminal ask, "Daddy, will Santa Claus still come to Hawaii?" Wiping the tear from her eye, her dad extended his arms to hug her and said, "Of course, Santa Claus will come to Hawaii. Santa delivers presents all over the world." She seemed to feel better, but was still extremely concerned that Santa would not know where she was. She further questioned her dad, asking him if they could overnight a letter explaining her whereabouts to Santa. I chuckled to myself; she was so cute. I hoped Santa Claus would give that little girl a great Christmas.

The boarding announcement bellowed over the loudspeaker,

calling for us to take our seats on the plane. I sat down, got comfortable, and listened to the airplane noise. I'm not sure what it is, but I love the adrenaline rush, the excitement before takeoff. It gives me a sense of adventure, of leaving all my troubles behind and embarking on a new journey.

I heard the stewardess make her safety announcements and tell us to buckle our seatbelts. The airplane sped across the runway, gradually lifting its nose as it pierced into the wild, blue yonder. I loved it! My stomach bottomed out and I could feel the rush as we sailed through the clouds.

I was very excited to go to Hawaii. However, at the same time, it didn't feel right because Mom wasn't there. I missed her and wished she could have been on the trip with us. I think that deep down, we were all feeling it. But Dad was determined to make the best of it, and he convinced us to do the same. It was our turn to have fun together, just the boys!

We had a long, seven-hour trip ahead of us. Wes and I played cards, listened to music, watched a movie, and were not even halfway there yet. I tried to talk my dad into letting the stewardess give me one of the mai tais they were passing out. I was underage, so of course Dad wasn't for it. Wes tried convincing me I looked twenty-one, suggesting I ask the stewardess myself so that we could then share the festive drink. Nice guy; he let me do the dirty work! However, I took it as a challenge. I noticed my dad had left his seat and made his way to the little mini-bar they had on the upper level. I figured he went for a mai tai, but actually, he was talking with the flight attendants about a surprise he was planning—a surprise I would never have believed if I hadn't seen it myself!

The stewardess began to walk over to where Wes and I were sitting. Without Dad around, this was my chance! I had her in view, and all I had to do was casually ask for a mai tai when she walked by. As she approached, I said in a deep voice, "Excuse me Miss. May I have a mai tai, please? She looked at me curiously and politely said she would be back in a moment. What did that mean? Was I in or did I get denied? As I waited, Wes perked up, making wagers and contemplating whether or not I was going to get my hands on Hawaii's most traditional drink.

Then it happened! My dad had told us about his surprise a week before we left for Hawaii, but Wes and I had laughed at him, never believing he could actually be serious. And yet there he was, making his way to the front of the plane as the children cheered and the parents looked baffled. They turned their heads and there he stood, with his white beard and plump belly, bellowing a jolly "Merry Christmas!" Santa Claus! It was the first time I had ever seen Santa in mid-flight.

Everyone on the plane looked on with amazement. The flight attendants, mystified at how the passengers loved it, relished in the Christmas spirit. Santa shook hands with all of the passengers, giving the kids candy canes and Christmas treats from his gift bag. He stole the show! But it didn't stop there. After Santa made his rounds, he pulled out Christmas carol song sheets, enough for almost every passenger on the plane. The airplane came alive as the passengers sang out, "Deck the halls with boughs of holly, fa la la la la, la la la la. 'Tis the season to be jolly, fa la la la la, la la la la…."

Everyone continued to sing traditional Christmas carols, led by the jolly St. Nick himself, as they sipped on mai tais while thousands of feet above the ocean, on their way to a tropical paradise. This went on for over an hour. I have never seen or heard anything like it. I have to admit that as embarrassed as I was, it was fun! Wes and I were actually laughing together again—laughing hysterically, and it felt good.

The response was phenomenal. After Santa Claus made his departure, people on the flight came over to shake my dad's hand, thanking him for such a great time. One gentleman came up and said he had traveled around the world by plane—in fact, had spent most of his time in the air —and had never in his life had a flight like this one! Then, to my amazement, along came the father of the little girl I had overheard in the terminal. He said he wanted to thank my dad because his daughter had been so worried Santa Claus would not come to Hawaii, and that when he appeared, she was in awe and more excited than ever. He said, "You have made my little girl's Christmas. Thank you!"

My dad was touched, as was I, by the overwhelming appreciation from everyone on the plane, not to mention the participation. The Christmas spirit was truly alive that day! I told Dad he was absolutely nuts! The word 'crazy' just wasn't strong enough. He looked at me and said, "Son, if I have learned anything in these past two years, it is to just be myself. Sometimes life is not fair, but no matter what, life will always be what you make it!"

I smiled as I pondered my dad's message. Then surprisingly, the stewardess appeared with complimentary mai tais. She said the flight attendants had so much fun with Santa that they would make one Christmas exception. Party time!

CHAPTER FOUR

In the Middle of the War

"When you go through life, always remember … you can only control what is in your control!"

~Darren McKenna

Things got ugly. A new phase in my journey had begun. I was caught in the middle of my parents' crossfire, trying to control the whirlwind of the "he said, she said" game of conflict. All kinds of unfamiliar terms—like legalities, divorce papers, child support, spousal support, custody, rights, court, judge, boyfriend, girlfriend, debt, and splitting assets—swept into my life like a tornado!

After years of keeping their problems private, my parents decided to break their rule of fighting behind closed doors. They began to express their feelings out in the open with no holds barred. Needless to say, it resulted in many explosive situations! I was left in an awkward position and often found it difficult to control my own anger and the hurt I felt when my parents verbally bashed each other.

During the fighting, both Mom and Dad began to ask me many questions about each other, such as: What is your dad doing now? Does your mom have a boyfriend? Is your dad still working at…? What did your mom say about…? At first, these questions appeared to reflect their sincere concern for each other. In reality, though, they were like sparks waiting to ignite as I related the answers back. I felt as though I was standing in the middle of the burning fire of my parents' rage. After awhile, it became evident that I had to be careful how I presented information to them. I was always in fear of a fight lurking in the background or of spending the rest of the night defending one of my parents to the other. It killed me to see the pain on their faces when they learned things they didn't want to hear.

The hurtful comments didn't stop there. As the pain and confusion of the divorce rippled throughout my extended family, some of them also indulged in speaking poorly of my parents. I took their comments very personally, whether they were true or not. Their words cut deeply and hurt worse than when my parents said distasteful things about each other. My parents created me. They helped make me who I am, and I am a part of them both. Therefore, an attack on either one of them felt like a direct attack on me, leaving me wondering whether or not I shared the same unfavorable characteristics. I couldn't understand whether I was bad or somehow wrong by being like or loving either of my parents. It was almost like I was supposed to choose sides—to blame one of my parents for the hurt, hardships, and chaos the divorce caused. It felt as though I should choose to hate one of them for it while I loved the other. I just wanted it to be okay to love them both, so that I could look in the mirror and love myself when I saw both of them staring back at me.

I was often too scared to confront my parents or other family members about the anger I felt when they made harsh accusations and remarks. I was taught to respect my elders. Therefore, I didn't want to deliberately offend any of them, and I worried that speaking about how I felt might sound disrespectful or rude. At the time, I didn't know how to express myself appropriately, so I bottled the feelings inside and convinced myself it didn't bother me.

Ignoring my feelings ended up making me miserable for reasons I couldn't explain. I became caught in a slow, steady cycle of self-destruction. All of a sudden, my anger turned inward and I became upset with myself for not being able to deal with what was happening around me. The anger spun me in so many directions that I couldn't see straight. As my frustration continued to climb, and just when I thought things couldn't possibly get any worse, *smack!* Someone or something would push me too hard, to a point where it became way too much and I felt like I was free-falling into a bottomless pit. At those moments, I could no longer bottle up my anger. I needed to explode and release the immense pain. I ended up unleashing some of my own vicious verbal attacks, laced with profanity and pain-inflicting comments! In the end, these outbursts solved nothing, and instead created much resentment and bitterness.

This period of time was unbearably difficult for everyone involved, and being civil seemed impossible. After a divorce, parents, family members, and children are left in severe crisis, pain, and grief. The situation creates a breeding ground for people to blame and go after each other blindly, not realizing how their comments and actions are affecting everyone. However, destructive as this phase may be, I also believe it is unavoidable and that it becomes a big part of the journey. It helps us learn about ourselves and grow, because these situations continue to push us past our limits as we seek a way to make peace. Life is not always black and white, and sometimes we need to mix up many colors to make a rainbow. We are and always will be emotional creatures who need to express our feelings, both good and bad. I truly believe that some things simply have to get worse before they can get better. It became important for me to realize that the only thing I could control was my own reactions to what happened. No matter how much I wanted to make my parents or family members do this or that, I couldn't.

Today, I still hold pain inside and some issues may never get completely resolved. I decided not to personalize every little comment I heard, because when you think about what other people say, it really tells you more about them than about who you are. In a divorce, parents, children, and family members all need time to vent—to be allowed to be angry, cry, hurt, and love. I believe the conflict leads us to learn how to react to these situations appropriately and how to take responsibility for ourselves rather than worrying about everyone else's actions.

Unfortunately, things get said that we end up regretting and sometimes can't take back. I don't believe that my parents had any direct intention of hurting me, nor did I of hurting them, yet unnecessary comments cut deep and left gaping wounds in all of us.

Even today, after thirteen years, certain callous remarks still enrage me. I harbor resentment to a degree where I have chosen not to talk about my mom, dad, or some of my extended family with certain people, because it's easier. I can't change people, and the truth is I don't want to feel pressured to hate the people I love. I want to love them for the good things about them. I learned my boundaries and also how to respect others. I had to find the courage to take a stand and politely ask people to refrain from making inappropriate remarks. I felt that we should either talk in respect of each other or not talk about it at all.

Over time, some issues become private and we can lock them away in a safe place, making our own peace with them. Other issues, whether we like it or not, eventually need to be faced. I know that even after I finish writing my book, there will still be some things that continue to haunt me. If we don't go back to heal our wounds and resolve certain issues, they will continue to linger in our lives. However, the more steps we do face, the more pieces we put together in our journey toward healing.

Making it Legal

The time came when my parents' separation evolved into the signing of divorce papers, making it legal and very final. Leading up to that point, my parents had to make many strenuous decisions—who gets what, who does what, who has custody, who pays what, who keeps what debt, and in the end, who ultimately comes out better in the wash.

I tried my best to stay out of the legal battles and various divorce settlements. It was easier on me and besides, even though I had opinions about different issues, it wasn't my job to deal with them or fix things. I always hated the idea of sitting in a courtroom, looking up at a judge who had the power to dictate the fate of my family, as though we were just part of some statistic. I didn't want anything to do with it. I figured my parents should be able to work things out fairly between themselves. However, I quickly learned that, when you're in the middle of a war, some form of mediation isn't such a bad thing. It helps to have someone ensure a certain level of peace and cooperation. Especially as anger raged between my parents and issues erupted, it became next to impossible to keep everyone's best interests in mind.

I remember when my parents signed the divorce papers. I felt like I had been blindsided, but it wasn't because my parents were making it legal and getting a divorce. It was something completely different that came along with it.

It was late in the afternoon, and I had just arrived home from school. I greeted Mom, who was sitting at the kitchen table with a pen in her hand. When I asked her how everything was going, she smiled and said, "Good." However, I could detect in her voice that something was on her mind, so I asked a second time, "Are you sure everything is okay, Mom? You seem flustered." She hesitated for a moment and then said, "Craig, come here for a second." I wasn't sure what was up, but I walked over to her and sat down at the table, waiting for her reply. I could see legal papers neatly piled beside her. Mom paused for a moment and said, "I want to let you know your father and I have filed for a divorce." That didn't really surprise me, since it felt like they already were anyway. However, I did get an empty feeling inside as I realized it was time to let go of that little spot I had reserved in the back of my heart for the possibility that perhaps, just maybe, my parents would reconcile.

What really got me was Mom's next announcement: "Craig, I also wanted to let you know that with the divorce, I decided to change my name. I need my own identity, so I took back my maiden name." I was stunned. It seemed like a reasonable thing to do, to want your own identity, but I felt my insides begin to tear, as I was unable to understand why Mom wanted to drop our family name.

Why is it that the tidal wave of divorce just keeps getting bigger and bigger? It seems just when you feel like you're making any kind of progress, *bang!* You get hit again! I really didn't want to feel any more pain at the time, or even think about asking her why, so I just said, "Okay, if that's what you want. If that's what you feel like you need to do, I guess it's fine with me." We talked briefly about the divorce procedures, and I never really did talk to her about why she changed her name.

I could deal with the divorce papers and the fact that it was final and legally over. It hurt, but I could handle it. However, I just didn't know how to handle Mom dropping our family name. I tried to forget about it, but it got under my skin and I couldn't explain why. On one hand, I understood how she could want her own identity and a new life. I wanted her to have that because it was important to her. Then, on the other hand, I had this ache in my stomach, hungry for an explanation as to why it was there. The truth lingering under my confusion was that I couldn't understand why Mom didn't want to have the same name as me, her son. It felt like she was embarrassed of our family, of me. I was so scared to know if that was even a little bit true, so I tried to avoid thinking about it. The strange part was that whenever someone mentioned her maiden name, it poked at me like a thorn in my side. Sometimes I wish Mom had kept the family name, because I guess I thought it would have kept a part of her connected to Dad. However, I know deep down that it was something she needed to do in order to move on, and that it had nothing to do with Wes or me. For that reason, I decided it was more important for me to honor her decision than to be selfish about it.

In a divorce, each parent may win a battle or two, but no one wins the war! Truthfully, I felt somewhat fortunate compared to the way things could have been. My parents, Wes, and I fought, yelled, screamed, hurt and scarred each other, but at the same time, we all worked towards finding ways to mend and help each other. There were also times when my parents made a conscious effort to inform us of some good things they still thought about each other. Dad always said the best thing he did for Wes and me was marry Mom. I thank my parents for that. I know it could have been worse, and I am grateful that I had the parents I did.

As children of divorce, we all have our own unique situations to bear. The divorce war can bring extreme consequences and additional serious circumstances such as alcohol problems, physical abuse, and even death threats. There are all kinds of obstacles to face. Whether or not one person is worse off, as children, parents, or family members, we all face the tremendous loss and hurt. The difference is in the way that we react to it.

The Fight

I faced many trying moments during this period, but none of them were as evident—and heated—as a certain fight I had with Dad. In the end, though, the episode taught me a valuable lesson and helped to make our relationship stronger.

I was at my dad's house, watching television, when the front door suddenly came crashing open and Dad bolted into the house, extremely upset. Obviously, he'd had another fight with Mom. The days had become utterly intense, and we were all dealing with many issues. The previous week had been especially excruciating for everyone. Dad was still denying the clear fact that things were absolutely over. He insisted on pretending it couldn't be true.

As Dad raged into the house, he ranted furiously, lashing out in sheer frustration about Mom and the whole divorce. In a panic, I followed him into the kitchen and asked, "Dad, what happened?" Not answering my question, he simply mumbled. I tried to ask him again, and he interrupted me with his cursing. I could only make out bits and pieces as I listened to his rants about how Mom could do this to him after seventeen years of marriage, how she could date some jackass, how she could bring issues up that happened years ago or accuse him of things that just weren't true, how she could pin the burden of fault on him, how we were falling into the poorhouse now, and so on. Standing there, trying to read Dad's mind, I found myself crippled with anger. Enraged with him for fiercely attacking Mom with his words and accusations, I was also incensed with Mom for doing this to him. I was completely torn and confused about what anything meant at that moment, and also about whose side I should be on. Lost, I didn't know what to do.

Dad was mad about virtually everything—the divorce, money, our family, this person, that person, his entire life. I tried to understand, but my anger continued to grow with each new comment from him. This was compounded by the fact that he was completely ignoring my questions, walking away from me anytime I approached him. The more he paced around the house, babbling in a rage, the more I realized how little I actually knew about my parents' relationship and why they had divorced. I wanted to know what was going on, and I began questioning whether or not my parents were still keeping many secrets from me. That feeling put me over the edge, and I lost it. My emotions began to erupt, and I shouted, "Dad, enough of this insane rambling crap! Tell me what's going on! Tell me what happened! Why are you keeping secrets from me? I am part of this, too!"

Dad looked at me, almost in disbelief. I had never really challenged him before. While growing up, I had found it difficult to talk to him or confront him about issues I was having. He could be very intimidating because of his sheer size, and talking back was typically a no-no in our household. Most times, I was scared to make him mad or embarrassed to talk about how I felt. Usually, I would go through Mom first and then she would talk to Dad. But this time was different. I was as mad as I've ever been, and we were standing in unknown territory where I could make up new rules. Petrified, I continued, "I want some answers, Dad! This is going nowhere if you don't talk to me!"

Looking for a response, I stared at him. He hesitated, looking back at me with bewilderment. Confused about something, he said in a calm but very sarcastic voice, "Craig, do you think I wanted this?

Do you think I asked for this to happen?" I was dumbfounded by Dad's statement and in no mood to listen to him act like the victim. It was my turn to let him know that I hurt, too! I threw the next punch as I yelled back, "What in the #$%! are you talking about, Dad? Do you think I wanted this? Do you think Wes wanted this? Do you think we asked for this? The whole thing is partly your fault! It's not all Mom's fault, you know!"

Wow! My dad came unglued and stormed upstairs, swearing. I quickly retreated to my bedroom and shut the door, scared and unprepared for the fight that was about to occur. Dad burst into my room within seconds.

Outraged and guilt-ridden, he opened with, "Craig, I didn't want this damn divorce. I don't want this for Wes or you. I would have done anything to change it if I could have! I would do anything to make it different—to be a family again!" I stood up and took the shouting match to a new level, as the word 'family' pierced my heart like an arrow.

"A family, Dad? What family? We don't have a family! I don't think we ever did! Nothing will ever be the same again!"

"What do you want me do, Craig? You tell me! I hate this whole divorce fiasco! I just can't believe everything we've had, everything we've been through, turned out like this!"

"Well, believe it, Dad! It happened! It's a freaking reality and you'd better get used to it, because it is not going away! I don't know what you want me to tell you to do. I didn't cause it!"

"Are you saying it's my fault? I caused this? For crying out loud, Craig, I am not the one who left! I didn't leave!"

"Well, you certainly had something to do with it, didn't you! What did you do, Dad? Why did Mom leave, then? All of a sudden she had some great desire to rip our family apart, leaving us desolate in the poorhouse, barely able to survive, just for the heck of it? What? She just thought she needed a change, huh Dad? What happened?"

Our voices roared out as we continued to lash out back and forth. We moved closer and closer to each other, shouting louder and louder about anything and everything, even if it didn't make sense and had no relevance whatsoever. Soon we came face to face, nose to nose, toe to toe in the peak of our anger! I could see my dad's muscles twitch and convulse, and I felt his breath on my face. I was frightened to death, but there was no way on God's green earth I was going to back down! My fists clenched and my body tightened. I was on the verge of taking a swing at him. As we shouted, I waited for the precise moment to strike. The energy was intense, and my heart raced so fast that I could feel it pounding through my chest. I screamed at the top of my lungs, "I can't take it anymore, Dad! The way you hang on! It's over! Mom left, damn it! She is gone and you are going nowhere like this. Dad, you are going nowhere, holding on. Give it up and get a life!"

Just before the first punch was about to be thrown, my words somehow hit Dad's weak spot. All of his bottled-up energy and emotions came to the surface as if a balloon had popped. He let go of his defenses as his arms fell to his sides and his chin dropped to his chest. He took one big deep breath, lifting his head to look at me. His eyes filled with tears, and without a word, he swung his arms around me, pulling me close to hug me tight. Paralyzed, we stood there, embraced, and cried! We cried for a long time.

After we were able to regain our composure, Dad and I talked. We talked about what we were both feeling about the divorce, and what we could do to help make things easier. That night changed our relationship for the better. It changed the impact of the divorce. It was one of the scariest moments in my life, but it broke through strong barriers between my dad and me. It became a first step toward building a loving relationship, one in which we could talk to each other about how we felt. To this day, I'm not exactly sure what the fight was truly about. However, whatever the reason, it brought us into a place where we could begin to feel the pain together. We realized that we were both hurting, and that we needed to listen to each other. For me, I needed to know it was okay to hurt, to have the right to be heard, and to speak out and voice my opinion. Although I can't speak for my dad, I believe in my heart that he needed to know I was there for him, supporting him, and that I loved him.

Who's The Parent Here, Anyway?

Like the fight I had with my dad, there were many times when I felt more like the parent. During a divorce, as parents hit crisis and war is declared, roles can easily become reversed. In order to make it through the journey, parents need support, help, understanding, and a chance to talk—just as much as children do. We need to be there for our parents as they are for us, but because of the degree of emotion involved, many times things become lop-sided. We can end up taking on the parenting role—consoling our parents, offering advice, caring for our brothers and sisters, and taking on extra responsibility.

It is vitally important to have balance. We each need a turn to talk and be heard, in order to work through the hurt, pain, issues, and emotions. At the same time, we need to grant others the same attention by comforting and listening to them. Otherwise, someone can end up with resentment, bitterness, deep-rooted anger, and eventually a lonely heart.

When my parents divorced, I had to grow up fast. With one swoop of the hand, I was forced to deal with adult problems. After the breakup, my parents became lost in their own cloud of pain, and my needs became forgotten and invisible. All of a sudden, I felt like the parent, as I was a shoulder to cry on and a supportive person to talk to. They were dealing with an overwhelming amount of problems all at the same time—years of issues, money difficulties, tough decisions, and a newfound freedom in their lives. It was hard to compete for attention. The divorce overpowered my world, and I was left taking responsibility for my parents' feelings and trying to ignore my own.

When it did come time that I needed a turn, when I needed my parents to listen to and comfort me, I found myself competing with the separate lives they hadn't even realized they were creating for themselves. I no longer felt that I could be a part of their individual lives. For instance, the August long weekend would come and my parents would be out on dates, instead of at the lake cabin, sitting around a bonfire with our family and friends.

I remember sitting in the old green rocking chair in the living room at Mom's house. I called it my thinking chair. Every time I felt confused or hurt, I would sit in my thinking chair and rock back and forth, listening to music as I contemplated my thoughts. It was a way for me to relax and release my feelings. As I sat there, I often debated where and how I fit into my parents' schedules. I didn't know when I was going to get any time with Mom or Dad to talk about or do the things I wanted to. It seemed as though every time I did see one of them, it would turn into a crazy kind of counseling session where I was being supportive and doing most of the listening. In turn, there just wasn't enough time for me. After awhile, this became too much, and I longed for us to simply do something together and have fun. Even though sometimes not spending so much time with my parents worked to my advantage, as any teenager will understand, eventually my need for time with them grew stronger and stronger.

As I sat there, pondering in my thinking chair, I realized that because I was so worried about my parents, I was not only losing out on fun time with them, but I was also neglecting my own feelings. I had become so busy taking responsibility for everyone else. I began to realize that it was crucial that I start to take responsibility for myself, and also take time for myself.

As children of divorce, we have the right to just be kids. It is the parents' responsibility to take care of us, whether or not that interferes with their private lives. I don't mean that I'm encouraging children to sabotage their parents' private time, especially as they begin to date, although I would be lying if I said I didn't try that! My point is that we need to take responsibility for ourselves and our needs. Children need a turn to be heard, to be cared for, to be supported, to do something fun, to deal with their emotions, and to hurt. Sometimes that means telling their parents straight out that they need time! It's important that we don't feel afraid to talk to our parents, even if it's just to tell them we want to watch a movie together, go to dinner, or play a game. Feelings are just feelings; they are not right or wrong. Things will sometimes be difficult and might not always work out. Therefore, be prepared to compromise, negotiate, and be flexible. Communication is the key.

Hidden Responsibilities

You know, even in the heart-wrenching battle to survive a divorce, in the midst of the war come some unique benefits children can take advantage of. These can include such benefits as more presents at Christmas or on birthdays, the chance to have two pets, occasional expensive gifts, more freedom to break curfew, and the opportunity to play one parent against the other is much easier! In my case, I only had to get one parent out of the house in order to host a party. Parents often overcompensate during and after their divorce because of the guilt they feel, a lack of time, or the other hardships divorce brings. They tend to be more inclined to overlook inappropriate behavior, so it becomes much easier to get away with things you would normally be punished for.

I believe that the benefits children of divorce can experience along the way are also an important part of the journey. They can arrive when we feel like we're immersed in darkness, reminding us that there is light at the end of the tunnel. They can help us cope and survive, and also give us a release or a break from the hurt and pain we feel. An example would be my trip to Hawaii. However, at the same time, we have to be careful of how much we take advantage of these benefits, especially when we know how easy it is for our parents to overcompensate. There can be enormous responsibilities and con-sequences hidden inside the benefits we seek or take advantage of.

It was late one night when Dad phoned me. He had been in a car accident. He had hit black ice on the highway, which sent his car spinning out of control. He crashed into a guardrail before sliding into the ditch, which probably saved his life. He wasn't seriously injured—just really shaken up. The accident hit a nerve in Dad, and he began to evaluate his life. He really didn't want to be out of town working all the time and then driving home late at night. The accident sparked a business idea in Dad's mind—a business Wes and I could do with him.

Dad, who had always been interested in the entertainment industry, came up with the idea of teaming up with me to perform an act from the movie "The Blues Brothers." We would impersonate Jake and Elwood at different functions. Along with this brainstorm, he planned to create a disc jockey business. This way we could incorporate the Blues Brothers act in our DJ performances, thereby bringing something unique to the marketplace. It sounded like a great idea, and it was a good opportunity for Dad, Wes, and me to spend some time having fun together. But at the same time, I truthfully thought it was just another one of Dad's ideas, and that we wouldn't end up doing it because of money, lack of time, or some other complication. I believed the idea would be forgotten.

Time went by, and nothing developed on the business idea until one rainy night when Dad and I had it out again. We were fighting about a comment he had made in which he suggested that Mom wasn't doing something she said she would. I stood tall and took Mom's defense as our shouting match got out of control. Finally, I let him have a low blow, stating, "Dad, it's not Mom who doesn't do what she says she will; it's you! You talk and talk about how we are going to do all of these things together, and then suddenly there is no time or no money, and we keep fighting about it over and over again! Dad … you are all talk and no action!" That absolutely enraged him, and he screamed at me, "Like what? What do I say I'm going to do that I don't? You tell me! Tell me one thing!" All that came to mind at the time to prove my point was the disc jockey business idea, so I suggested sarcastically, "What about your DJ business and Blues Brothers idea? Like that will ever happen! We will never get to do that!"

Dad walked out of the house without saying a word. Within one week, like a flash of lightning, I became a partner in a DJ business.

Dad handed me a newspaper ad that read, "Become a DJ! All the equipment you will need." Simply because of a misunderstanding and an unfinished conversation between Dad and me, he was starting up a business with money and time I knew he didn't have. He was overcompensating for the guilt he felt about broken promises, for my stubbornness and pain through the divorce, and for our lack of time together. He was also proving a point to himself and to me. All of this resulted in the conception of the "Blues Brothers Music Phenomenon." Without any research, money, extra time, disc jockey experience, or formal business plan—and without an office or storage facilities—we were in business.

Being absolutely naïve about the responsibilities that BB Music Phenomenon would bring, I was excited! I was spending more time together with Dad and Wes. I was enjoying the fact that I had my own business and could now expense the music I wanted to buy. I also now had an incredible sound system for entertaining! All I was seeing were the small benefits that came with the business. It was great! I had set up all the equipment in the basement, and I had a blast mixing music, creating light shows, entertaining friends, pretending I was on the radio, and hosting a few too many parties. The DJ business brought fun and benefits that I took advantage of, but it also brought a lot of responsibility that I wasn't ready for and found extraordinarily difficult to manage. I walked into a huge debt, and eventually I was going to have to work to pay for it!

I will never forget our very first gig, and I can laugh now at how ridiculous I must have looked. Wes and I were up on stage; I had a microphone in one hand as I was dancing around, staring at three hundred people. Some were half-drunk, and not all of them were dancing. Many were just staring at us, shouting and chanting out different song titles to play. In an attempt to get things going and create that DJ magic the crowd was looking for, Wes and I came up with what later became our slogan: "When in doubt, pull the Pointer Sisters out!" It worked, and the song "Jump" had everybody, young and old, up dancing, singing, and having a great time—until halfway through the song, when the tape deck began to eat the tape.

I panicked and reached over to stop it, spilling my drink all over the mixing board. The yelling and chanting of people demanding more music could be heard a block away! Oh, what a night! Basically, I had no clue what I was doing, and was trying to wing it. My voice crackled every time I announced the next dedication. Needless to say, I sought out professional advice as we continued in the business. Like most things, it became a huge learning curve and in many ways a battle all on its own, as I juggled late nights, girlfriends, work, family issues, social life, and school. This all happened because I couldn't simply tell my dad I wanted to spend time with him, or ask if he still loved me and was proud of me.

After four years, we sold the business. Despite some disasters, I became a much better DJ, and we developed a strong business—although truth be told, the Blues Brothers act could have used a little polishing. However, through my experience as a DJ and a business owner, I learned a tremendous amount about myself. I learned many life lessons the hard way, which I believe built stronger character in me. Experience is the greatest teacher. Most importantly, I realized how important communication is—that is, productive communication where we're not scared to talk about our true feelings.

When we make choices in life, it's important that we know we are solely responsible for the benefits and consequences each choice brings, good or bad. Had I known what the business was really going to be like, I would have never agreed to do it. However, at the same time, it ironically brought my dad and I closer together.

It wasn't just Dad who overcompensated. I also took advantage of the situation with my mom. Mom carried a burden of guilt after she left, and I believe she was scared to lay down the law with me for fear that she would hurt me. I wished she would just let go of her guilt.

I remember wishing she would just be a mom. At first, it became easy to take advantage of the situation and lash out at her or not listen to a word she said. That's what teenagers do, but the divorce made it even easier to play the guilt card and get away with everything. This included partying, drinking, sneaking out, staying out all night, and having a great time with all my newfound freedom. If my mom ever said anything about it, I would turn the attack on her. But that got old fast. After awhile, I realized what I really wanted was to know that she cared about me. I wanted her to put her foot down, set me straight, and prove she was looking out for my best interests. I'm not sure that would have been an easy task on her part, due to my attitude at the time. I wanted Mom to say, "Craig Henry! What did I tell you about that?!" I wanted her there, pushing harder instead of backing down, so that I could know she cared and loved me.

Divorce brings unique drawbacks and benefits. Again, each situation will be a little different. As far as the benefits go, we should enjoy the little ones for what they are but remember that the more we take advantage of the situation, the more responsibility we may bear in the end.

CHAPTER FIVE

Financial Crisis

*The only thing I needed to know through my parents'
divorce was that they loved me. I didn't need to know what
they fought about or who did what to whom. I didn't need
to know which one was to blame for the divorce. I just
needed to know that it wasn't me.* ~Joanne Keylor

M y parents had been separated for almost two years when
the real financial crisis broke and we were hit with hard
times! I was in the kitchen getting a bowl of ice cream
when Dad walked in through the back door of our house, the for-
mer family home, with John, a real estate agent. John was on a mission to finalize an appraisal of our home; he scanned each room and
quickly jotted down notes in his black notepad. Dad then asked him
to sit down at the table so they could discuss some details. Not wanting to get in the way, I walked into the living room to watch television. Contemplating Dad's motives, I suddenly became nervous. He
had mentioned that this day might come, but I wasn't willing to
believe that it was a reality.

John left, and I watched through the front window as he
pounded a "For Sale" sign into the ground. Turning my head in sorrow, I looked at Dad for an explanation. He hesitated as he walked
into the living room and sighed before saying, "Craig … son … I'm
sorry. I hung on as long as I could, but the time has come. I have to
sell the house."

Elaborating on that cold, hard fact, Dad informed me that
because we had lost the two-income family, and with the debt that

had accumulated through the years, he couldn't afford the house. Both he and Mom were seriously struggling, trying to make it on their own. The house had to be sold in order for us to survive. I was heartbroken. The home I was trying so desperately to hang onto, the home my family had worked so hard to purchase, was now going to be taken away because of the divorce. It was the last thing I wanted to let go of. I still didn't want to have to admit that my family really didn't exist anymore.

The Early Years

Our family's financial crisis actually started to develop a few years before my parents separated. As I look back, I honestly believe it was one of the major factors that contributed to the divorce. I was in grade three when Dad was transferred for work, resulting in our move to the small town I grew up in. Back then, times were good financially for my parents—not only good, but great. It was a new decade, the eighties—a booming period of time. Dad had a good job working for a tire company, making enough money to enable Mom to stay home with Wes and me. It was close to an ideal family situation. My parents were able to buy a nice house on a quiet corner lot, tucked away in a quaint crescent. However, because of the economic boom, they paid a hefty price.

The house was great. I met one of my closest friends three days after we moved in, as he lived on the other side of the street, just a few houses down. All of the families that lived in the crescent rallied together to make it a fun and happy place to live. My fondest memory, without a doubt, is of the endless games of hockey we played on our own private rink, built by the parents on an empty lot next door to my friend's house. It was very cool.

We lived there for four good years before the financial thunderstorm began to form and my parents took the brunt of skyrocketing mortgage rates. This sent my Mom back to work to help pay the bills and left our family with a lingering financial strain.

Through the economic shift, rates continued to climb and the strain eventually forced my parents to move us out of our familiar home. Mom and Dad were hit hard. They had bought our house at a high time in the real-estate market. As interest rates rose, the price of homes declined drastically, leaving my parents unable to afford the house. They incurred a significant loss on the sale of the home, which of course created a big debt. We moved into a small duplex with a rent price that we could afford at the time. It was in the same town, so Wes and I were able to stay in the same school. Looking back now, I can see how the sale of the crescent house really began to escalate my parents' problems. The agonizing financial stress and the fact that we now had to rent didn't help.

The decisions that my parents needed to make contributed to more and more problems. For instance, Dad could have declared bankruptcy at the time and walked away from the house, like many others did, but he decided against it because it would have ruined his credit rating. In hindsight, maybe it would have been a better thing to do, because they wouldn't have accumulated such a significant amount of debt. That one decision put enormous financial strain on my parents, causing intense disagreements and leading to situations like Dad not joining us on summer holidays at the lake because he had to work. Years later, he told me, "Craig, you know the old saying that absence makes the heart grow fonder? Well, I found it can also make your partner forget." I understand now what he meant by that statement, as his absence certainly did not bring my parents closer together. There are many things in life that are much more important than money. Financial stress, if not controlled, can eat at you in ways that make you a different person, and it can make you do things you normally wouldn't do.

Hidden Stress Builds Up

For me, one of the hardest parts of the whole divorce was the fact that our parents never let us kids know much about the things they were going through during those early years. They kept things hidden and were good at pretending everything was okay in their relationship. Not until after the divorce did we see the fine print at the bottom of the page. Wes and I only knew surface information, the fluff—not the actual truth and secrets that lay beneath. We were told things like, "Money is tight and we're going through a difficult time, but we will make it through." Nothing really clued us in to the depth of the problems that were happening.

It wasn't until the divorce that I started to learn who my parents really were. I'm not saying they should have told us everything, but from my perspective, I really felt betrayed and cheated that they didn't. For one thing, I had believed that Mom and Dad were working hard together to make things better—that we all were as a family, standing strong to get through a tough time. I was proud of that. I guess I feel that if I would have known how deep the problems went, I might have had the chance to help back then, before things got to the point of no return. Although it probably wouldn't have made any difference, I feel like I might have had the chance to speak up and say, "Dad, you have to come with us on our holiday trip or I'm not going," or ask, "Mom, what could I do to help make things better for you and Dad?"

Since that fateful day when our parents sat Wes and me down, I have been mad at myself for not seeing what was going on and realizing there was a potential danger. I felt like a fool, as though I was stupid for trusting in something I shouldn't have—not that it was ever my responsibility to. I guess that, as the oldest child, I have a strong need to try and protect everyone in my family, to know they are okay and safe. Sometimes even today, when I want to put my trust in something, it's a battle for me because I have a hard time letting go of the little devil that taps me on my back and screams, "Be careful!"

It had taken my parents many years, several moves, and hard work to be able to create the stability and security that came with the crescent house. It was the start of building a true foundation for our family.

When they lost it and had to rebuild everything again, they were tired—especially my mom. I distinctly remember her being fed up with all of the moving and consolidating of debt. Having to do all of this again contributed to many resentful feelings that I know my parents never truly dealt with.

As a family, we talked about how good it would be to get into a home again—to find stability and create roots. We made it a family goal, and I was old enough to understand that at the time. It took a few years of living in small rental duplexes, but when my parents were finally able to buy a house again, I saw it as a true family victory. We even repainted and remodeled the home to make it our own. I loved that house. It was perfect for our family, and I was so proud of Mom and Dad. This is why the house became so important to me.

I had a connection with that house, and for me it always stood as a symbol of my family's triumph. Even today, when I drive by and look at the house, I only remember the good times we had there as a family. When my parents bought the home, the whole experience taught me a valuable lesson about money and how to persevere. Mom and Dad showed me the importance of having a goal and never giving up.

Learning the Value of Money

I put the lesson my parents taught me into practice when I decided I wanted to buy a trampoline for our backyard. This would become my own personal victory.

Trampolines had come onto the market and were selling like hotcakes. My cousins had one, and I wanted one in the worst way. The only problem was that they were very expensive and Dad told me he couldn't afford it. However, he also said that if I used my own money, I could buy one. I wasn't too keen on his suggestion, because at twelve years old, I only had a dollar and twenty cents in my piggy bank. About a week later, Dad and I happened to go to the bottle depot to cash in the bottles that had been piling up in the back shed. I saw my opportunity there and as we drove home, I asked, "Dad, did you mean it when you said I could buy the trampoline with my own money?" Without really thinking, he chuckled to himself and said, "Sure, Craig. When you earn a thousand dollars, you can buy a trampoline." I ignored his sarcasm and decided it was time to put my idea into action.

My goal was to collect bottles until I had enough money to make my purchase. It was the month of June and school was almost out for summer. I launched my plan and began to walk around town looking for empty bottles. I worked harder than I ever had before, every day after school for over two weeks. I collected what I thought to be a mountain of bottles just in time for summer holidays. I was ecstatic, because I believed without a doubt that I would have enough money for the trampoline. I showed Dad my stash of beer bottles, cans, and plastic pop bottles. Impressed by my efforts, he congratulated me, but said, "Craig, I think before you get your hopes up, you should take the bottles to the depot and see how much money you actually have." It felt like Christmas Eve as I anticipated that the fruits of my labor would bring me the trampoline on the brochure—the one that I stared at every night before bed, dreaming of landing the perfect backflip. I felt a sense of pride about my accomplishment as I unloaded the bottles—that is, until the cashier placed one hundred and eighty-seven dollars in my hand. It was a far cry from the amount of money I needed for the trampoline.

The next week, I did nothing except mope around, depressed about the reality of the situation. I wondered how I could possibly get enough money before the end of summer. I rallied Wes and some friends to help me continue to collect bottles, hoping this would speed things up. However, the friends soon became bored and it was just Wes and me. Time was slipping away, and I realized I needed to be more resourceful and find an efficient way to speed things up. I started asking myself how I could get my hands on more bottles in less time. Then I remembered how the Boy Scouts went door to door on bottle drives. August was just around the corner, so I started to go from house to house with my old red wagon, explaining that I was saving up for a trampoline. I asked if I could be of service and help clear space in people's garages or sheds by taking their empties off their hands. That worked much better, until I clued in to the idea that I could get even more bottles if I posed as a Boy Scout. Mom put a stop to that idea quickly, though, and I was back to walking the town.

By the first week of August, I had only raised a little over four hundred dollars. I was too frustrated to continue and didn't know what to do; I needed a better plan. My parents saw my frustration and, probably because they couldn't stand to listen to me talk about the trampoline constantly, they came to talk to me. They told me that in the beginning, they had thought trampolines were too dangerous. However, they saw that I had been making an incredible effort and that I had shown I could be responsible. They said that if I could come up with half of the money, they would help out with the rest. This was the little extra push I needed. It rejuvenated my quest and I went looking for bottles, more determined than ever!

With a little over two weeks left in the summer, I had finally earned my half. I will never forget the day I came home from a friend's house on my bike, expecting to later go to the store and buy the trampoline. Instead, Dad had decided to surprise Wes and me. I dropped my bike on the driveway as I noticed Dad waving his arm from the backyard, calling me to come and see. There it was! It was fourteen feet in diameter, with black mat meshed together and chrome surroundings with decorative green and yellow padding. I don't know what was more shocking—the look on Dad's face when he found out that Wes and me had actually raised half the money, or the look on mine when I saw the trampoline. I felt victorious as I climbed aboard for the very first jump. Excited, I whispered to myself, "I did it!"

The day that I found out Dad was selling our family home, my heart broke. But it wasn't just the house that sold. A week before we were to move out, Dad had an open house for a liquidation sale. Almost everything went. Most of the furniture was sold, as well as our television, pictures, some of our weights, and—a devastating blow for me—the trampoline. That was an ultimate crusher! As I watched the people who bought it disassemble the pieces and take it away, it felt like someone had reached in, grabbed my heart, and twisted it back and forth. I couldn't talk about it with Dad. I tried to just pretend like it never happened. But that was the icing on the cake for me as I packed my remaining things, feeling completely destroyed. Dad tried to comfort me by promising that one day we would get it all back.

I stood in the entrance of my bedroom, holding my suitcase and looking at the emptiness. I felt empty inside too, watching the memories melt away. It felt like my life had started to disappear. As I stood there, I closed my eyes and prayed to God, demanding an answer to why I had to go through this. Did I deserve this? Did I do something wrong? My eyes began to water as the words slipped from my mouth, "God, please let there be one day in my life where I can feel like I really won." Tears flooded my face as I walked down the stairs and said goodbye to my home.

My First Real Job

The financial crisis forced me to find my first real job. Dad was a friend of one of the local restaurant owners, so he managed to arrange an interview for me to work in one of the most profitable divisions of the restaurant, pizza delivery. I was the pizza delivery boy unless it was a slow night, and then I became the errand boy. On those nights, it was my responsibility to wash dishes, grate cheese, mop floors, and keep the storage areas tidy. I can't say I was overly thrilled about the work, but I enjoyed my co-workers.

Working at the restaurant helped me make it through this tough time. After the house sold, money was very tight. Dad had taken a new job working out of town, and he had the bulk of my parents' debt to pay off. I went to live with Mom, who had decided to venture back to school and work on the degree she needed in order to move ahead at her workplace. That proved to be bad timing, adding more strain to the financial crisis and leaving virtually no extra resources for Wes or me. I became a part of the working community. My pizza delivery tips and paychecks were my means of survival. The restaurant also had one extra benefit that proved to be vital for me. Each night that I worked, I was allowed to have one meal off the menu as a bonus. I needed it, especially with the size of my appetite, which I had inherited from Dad. The extra meal helped take the bite out of my hunger.

I had been working at the restaurant for a few months when our family fell deep into poverty for about an eight-month period. It was a very difficult time. Without some help from our family, I'm not sure if my parents, Wes, or I would have made it through as well as we did. Mom couldn't afford to spend much on groceries; she bought just the bare essentials. However, with both of us boys living there, the two small TV dinners, apple, carrots, and box of baking soda that sat in the fridge just didn't cut it. Dad was out of town most of the time, and with his bills to pay for, he too had little to spare. Many nights, Wes and me were still hungry when we left the supper table. Needless to say, asking for expensive clothes was out of the question. I was grateful to have had the convenience of the restaurant. Without it, there were a few days when I'm not sure what I would have done, because I know I would have been too proud to ask for help.

I was very embarrassed of my situation, but in order to get through it, I had to do some things that today I'm not so proud of. Working at the restaurant just didn't provide enough money to cover my everyday expenses. My tips were going to pay for the gas I needed to deliver pizza, and my paychecks were for buying food and some essentials. Trying to keep up, I had to come up with some moneymaking alternatives.

To make extra money, I started my own bottle-stealing ring at the restaurant. It would have been easier just to steal money from the pizza deliveries, but for some reason I didn't think that was right or ethical—and yet I could rationalize stealing empty cases of beer bottles from the back shed. I would never take much—only enough so that my boss wouldn't be suspicious. I'm sure he checked the shed, although he never said anything to me about the missing cases.

The other thing I did was sneak soup, salad, and pizza when I was hungry. I didn't feel right about that, however, so many times I would instead finish off the half-eaten meals that came back on plates to be washed. I would cut off the untouched portions of steak, potatoes, fish, or hamburgers, because otherwise it would just be thrown out anyway. I know it sounds gross, but believe me, when you are hungry, you will eat whatever you can find. One day, a table sent back six uneaten lobsters because they were cold. I couldn't believe it, so I ate them all. I didn't care; to me, it was like a treat. I never once told my parents about this, because I know it would have hurt them deeply. I was too proud to ask for help, so I had to learn to survive—and I did.

Fortunately, it wasn't too long before my parents started to bounce back. Unfortunately, though, Mom had to quit school and go back to work in order to get back on her feet again. Dad started to build a stronger income with his new job, and that enabled him to help out more. During that eight-month period, I really learned how to be humble, especially when many of my friends came from wealthy families, and their biggest concern was how many pairs of designer jeans they should buy.

My struggles during this difficult time taught me about humility. I believe that we all need to learn to laugh at ourselves at least once in a while. Life will bring us many adventures and sometimes we need to suck up our pride in order to make it through. These challenges teach us to endure and learn never to give up. Sometimes it is a hard road, and we are bound to make mistakes along the way, but in the end, we will be able to look back and know that we are better for the lessons we learned.

The Hockey Dream Dies

It was a realization that couldn't be avoided and a decision I regret. I elected to quit playing hockey. Many factors contributed to my decision, including the pressure and guilt I felt about burdening my parents with the expense. There was also the fact that my performance had sunk to an all-time low, coupled with my diminishing self-esteem. The biggest mistake I made was to let my constant fear to ask my parents for help get in the way of pursuing my dream.

I remember the day the dream began. I was seven years old, and I had won my first trophy in an Atom hockey tournament. My team won first place, so we all received trophies. I loved that trophy. To me, it was like the Stanley Cup. It had a white marble base with a decorative, gold plastic hockey player mounted on top of a ruby-red, diamond-shaped shaft. Every time I looked at the trophy, I could see myself skating alongside Wayne Gretzky as I scored the winning goal with only seven seconds left in game seven of the Stanley Cup series!

I took my trophy everywhere I went, until one fateful night. Wes and me were putting on our pajamas and getting ready to watch a movie before bed. Mom called us from the kitchen to say the popcorn was ready. I raced out of my room and down the hall with my trophy in hand, when suddenly, Wes burst out of his room and we collided. My trophy flew through the air and broke upon impact with the ground. Mom came running into the hall, frantic as she pulled me off of Wes, who was starting to turtle in fear of the punch I was about to land on him. Mom yelled, "Craig Henry! What on earth are you doing?" I shouted, "But Mom, Wes broke my trophy!" Grabbing me by the arm, she said, "Craig, it was just an accident. We can glue it back together. Why are you getting so upset?" I looked at her with a small tear in my eye and said, "Because, Mom, I worked my whole life for that trophy!"

It was my first year of midget hockey. I started the season playing Midget AAA for a city team close to our small town. Tryouts were in September, when school started. It felt good to get back on the ice and it put new excitement and vitality back into me. But that turned out to be short-lived. I became overcome by the idea that I might have to quit. It was expensive to play, and my family was knee-deep in financial crisis. I tried to forget about all of the worries that were surrounding me—lack of money, the divorce, school, family pressures, and all of the other things teenagers go through. I tried not to worry about anything and just play hockey, but I was changing. I was going through so many emotional changes that my mind wasn't on hockey anymore. Also, the fact that we couldn't afford it was really playing on me.

Hockey tryouts started out great. I was energized just to play again, and the coaches were impressed with what they saw in me. I was poised to be a shoe-in for the team. As the regular season drew closer, my family life became like walking on a tightrope, as issues regarding the divorce collided with the financial crisis. It became too hard. There was fighting, yelling, blaming, and lots of crying. Depressed, I began to give up on myself completely—not just in hockey, but in school and with friends and girlfriends. I put forth little or no effort. My confidence was gone and I started to believe I wasn't worth much.

My dream was slipping through my fingers and I couldn't stop it. I started to feel like I didn't deserve to be a professional hockey player. In competitive hockey and sports, coaches, teammates, and fans don't care if you're hurting, upset, or having a bad day. They expect and demand your best performance always—something that I knew in my heart I couldn't give anymore. I knew the reality was that I wasn't measuring up, but I didn't care. I gave up on caring about myself. I just wanted to avoid everything, hang out with friends, drink, and party. I wanted to forget everything that was important to me, because I started to believe it would just be taken away anyway, so what was the use. I developed a strong and destructive attitude.

For many reasons, I let go of the dream before I was able to give it an honest chance. I felt I was putting too much pressure on my parents with what it cost to play, and I was too afraid to ask for their help. I was afraid they would try to do anything they could to keep me playing hockey. I didn't want the guilt of disappointing them if I couldn't perform. I was scared to let them know that I had quit believing in myself, or that I didn't feel good enough. I had become a coward, letting myself be defeated before someone else could take it away from me instead.

It wasn't long after the regular season had begun when the coach took me aside and said he had no choice but to cut me. Stating his disappointment in me, he said, "People talk about you as this great hockey player. What happened? You started out with a great camp, and now you couldn't pass a donut. It's like you're going through the motions out there, like you've given up!" He shook his head and said he had to do what was best for the team, and obviously I wasn't there to play hockey. I knew it was coming, but it hurt all the same. The coach was right. I had given up on myself and quit.

To this day, I will never know if I made the wrong decision. It hurt so badly to give up on my dream that, even after ten years, I have never played hockey again. I regret quitting for many reasons, and the biggest is that now I have to live with the fact that I will never know if I could have played in the NHL. Even if I had tried but didn't make it in the end, at least I would have known that I gave it my best shot. I could have been proud of that.

I made two big mistakes when I gave up my dream. One, I gave up on myself as I wallowed in self-pity. Two, I didn't ask for help when I really needed it. I didn't know that it was okay to ask my parents to help out—that I wouldn't have been a burden. I didn't know at the time that I deserved the best in life, just like everyone else.

In the end, I lost and sold myself out because of fear. I watched as some of my friends and teammates were drafted to the NHL. I learned the importance of having a dream, and I will never let go of it again—even though now it takes on a different shape.

Choosing One Way or Another

Every so often, life will bring us to a crossroads, challenging us to debate the direction of our future and presenting us with options to choose from. These are the precious moments that usually we fear—yet they have the ability to completely reshape our lives and create our destiny.

Hitting bottom is a scary place to be. Giving up and throwing away all hope is even worse. I realized that one night as I sat in jail in a drunken stupor, pondering where my life was headed. I had given up on myself, quit hockey, felt worthless, had no money, and saw no light at the end of the tunnel. I had given in to my fears, and began to find pleasure only when I escaped with alcohol. As a teenager, it was common to drink and party. It was a part of growing up. However, there came a period of time for me when drinking wasn't just about having a good time with friends. It became about drinking as much as I could in order to send my painful feelings into oblivion. I didn't want to feel; I just wanted to forget.

The night started out innocently enough. I wanted to develop phase two of the party room by adding an addition to the bar my friends and I had built. My idea was to create a basketball game similar to the arcade versions where you shoot hoops and the ball rolls back. The only problem was that I had no building materials. Some of my friends had gathered in the party room to have a few drinks, and we got engrossed in a conversation about the construction of the basketball game. After about a case of beer and half a twenty-six of Silent Sam vodka, we prepared a strategy to obtain our building materials. First, we headed to another friend's house to continue the party. Between shots of rye, my friend Jack and I kept talking about building the basketball game, until we became so drunk that we decided to launch our magnificent plan that night.

We figured that all we needed was wood, and with so many new houses being developed in our town, no one would miss a few pieces here and there. We called it "Operation Wood Find." To complete our mission, we needed to secure a getaway driver, because Jack and I could barely walk up the stairs. With our charm and grace, we were able to talk our friend Pam into being the driver. Although we thought we were being so strategic, I am sure Pam only agreed to it because she was concerned about getting Jack and I home safely.

We jumped into Jack's car and set out. As we approached the new developments, we searched for two-by-fours or small sheets of plywood, but all we could find were sixteen-foot two-by-sixes, which we didn't need. However, not willing to be defeated, Jack and I decided to stack as much wood as we could fit into the car anyway. We had to hang the boards six feet out of the window in order for them to fit. Foolishly, we told Pam, "Hit it," Then we sped away from the scene of the crime, with maybe a whopping total of twenty dollars' worth of wood in our possession.

Soon, we heard sirens echoing in the background and noticed red and blue police lights flashing in the rearview mirror. Scared, Pam stopped the car. The police officer asked all of us to climb out and put our hands up on the roof of the cruiser. The officer searched us, placed us under arrest for theft, and hauled us down to the police station. He threw Jack and me in jail while they interrogated Pam. I couldn't believe we received the whole nine yards for something so stupid, but I guess we did commit a crime. I felt so badly, not because I was sitting in jail, but because I had brought two friends in there with me. I was especially sorry about Pam; her motives were only to be a good friend and watch out for Jack and me.

About a half-hour went by before Jack and I were brought in for questioning. In the meantime, the police had called our parents. Eventually, Jack and Pam were sent home. The officers threw me back in jail, explaining that since I had been the instigator of the crime, I would be the only one charged. Panic set in as I sat in jail, terrified, until the next morning.

I never found out the truth about why I was really sitting alone in a jail cell all night, scared out of my mind, until probably seven years later. When the police had called my mom, they'd informed her about what we did and suggested that they weren't very concerned, as we weren't hardened criminals. They said that she could come and pick me up. However, Mom, concerned about my excess drinking, asked if they would keep me there overnight to teach me a lesson.

It was a lesson learned indeed. To me, the police made it out like I should get used to sitting in the jail cell, as I was going to be prosecuted. So many thoughts crossed my mind—where my life was headed, what I really wanted, and how I had ended up in that situation. I couldn't believe something that seemed so ridiculous had the potential to ruin my life. It made me take a hard look at myself and question what I was choosing to become. I thought to myself, *Well, Craig... where do you want your life to go? Have you given up completely? Do you really want to end up in here?* I knew that I didn't want to continue on the road I seemed to be heading down—that I wanted to change and make things better. I was staring at a crossroads, trying to decide what path to take. I decided to take the more difficult route—to make something of my life by finding things I liked about myself and starting to eliminate those I didn't.

Until that night in jail, I had forgotten about my right to choose. I was so focused on my emotions, feeling like I had lost everything. I had hit rock bottom and felt like I had run out of choices to make things better. I was escaping my pain and trying to forget by drinking. All I wanted to do was curl up in a little ball and blame the world for what I had lost. As I sat in jail, drenched with the awful smell of alcohol, it was like a lightening bolt hit me. I realized where the choices I had been making were leading me, and I knew that the other choice I had was to face reality.

In my opinion, choosing one way or another—or more appropriately, choosing to face it or forget—is the most challenging part of the divorce journey. In our lives, we sometimes find ourselves faced with the choice to grow, face our fears, accept our vulnerability, and move on—or to avoid dealing with things, temporarily escaping the pain but letting it linger inside. The important thing to remember is that we need to eventually face our demons, or they will live on to enslave and control us.

It is easy to fall into the trap of escaping or denying your feelings. This sometimes involves abusing alcohol, drugs, sex, or people. We choose to take what appears to be the easy way, because it seems simpler than facing our feelings and fears. Unfortunately, when we do that, we eventually also lose all hope and find ourselves drowning in confusion. The farther we go down that road, the more likely it is to lead to serious danger for ourselves and those around us. The farther we fall into the hole of avoidance, the longer it takes and the harder it is to choose another path and climb out. I learned that the faster you can take ownership of your mistakes, the faster you will be able to move on in the direction you want to go. We all need to start somewhere.

Finding Security

Being faced with poverty was one of the worst feelings I have ever experienced. Everything got cut back and our standard of living spiraled downwards. Only the basic necessities were important, and it wasn't the future I was worried about anymore, but simply how I was going to make it through the day.

Our family went through the serious part of our financial crisis for close to a year, until my parents started making more money and accepted some help from family members. Throughout the struggle, I began to obsessively seek security and stability in my life. I realized the importance of money and how it can have a strong control over people. Before all of this, my family had been doing well, and Wes and me were used to a nice lifestyle. It was nothing fancy, but we lived well. Then suddenly, we didn't have a lifestyle—we were simply surviving! I longed for security, to feel safe and not have to worry about money. It seemed like it was all I began to think about—the need for money. I hated the control it had over me.

Once I had been working for some time, I was able to start saving and vowed that I would never again find myself without money.

I started to associate money with security and stability. I became obsessed. I needed to have money if I ever wanted to have a future. I was that way for a long time, with all of the moving around and sacrifices we had to make. As I lost some of my belongings and we lost the house, I worried that I would never find security again. I even had an overwhelming need to hang onto possessions I owned, for fear that someone would take them away.

It took many years before I felt secure; in fact, it was not until I was married. The interesting part is that I created the stability and security in my life. I hadn't depended on anyone else to provide it for me. I realized that true security doesn't lie in having money—real security lies within a person. Even today, I am still conscientious about money, but I look at it differently.

The thing I hated most during those difficult times was the control that money had over my family. It was always an excuse for why we couldn't have things, be things, own things, do things, and try things. I hated it! And I still do. Today, I have been able to break down that barrier, and I believe that I control the money in my life, instead of it controlling me and making me do crazy things. I control my own security.

Since I have changed my attitude towards money, more has come into my life, and I have found the gateway to security and stability. After all I went through, I now believe that money provides us stability by meeting our basic needs. However, finding security in life goes beyond money. It comes from within. We are as secure in our lives as we are in ourselves! The more we feel secure in our abilities, talents, and self-image, the easier it becomes to obtain money and financial well-being. I found security within myself, and I now know that if I am ever faced with adversity or another financial crisis, I will survive.

CHAPTER SIX

The Strength Within

"It is during our moments of weakness, through grief and despair, that we realize our strength."

~Celine Sirois

I believe that all children who have to walk the journey through their parents' divorce are extremely courageous. There is an old saying that defines the word courage: "In the presence of danger, courage is not the absence of fear, but rather, facing the danger in the presence of fear." It takes mountains of strength and pillars of courage to face the enormous heartache and loss associated with a divorce. It takes even more courage to grab hold of life and make it everything you want it to be despite the uncontrollable circumstances divorce brings. Even though as children we don't have a choice about our parents' decision to part ways, we can control our reactions and make choices about the impact it has on our lives.

Somewhere within our hearts, we all have a little spark that is capable of igniting our courage to take control of our lives at our weakest moments! That strength within allows us to face our fears, confront our pain, and find the spirit to better our lives. Before I could really grasp the effects of my parents' divorce, in order to make a positive difference in my life, I had to find that little spark!

It's Okay to Be Me

I decided to play for my high school's basketball team, which turned out to be a horrendous experience and probably an all-around bad choice. However, life seems to teach us what we need to know even when we aren't aware that we need it. Dad keeps telling me that everything happens for a reason, and in this case, I guess it did.

At the time, I was having difficulty connecting with my friends at school because of how I had changed through the divorce. I was lost, my reputation was crumbling, my spirit was gone, and I wasn't much fun to be around. I felt that I couldn't simply go and talk to my friends to reconnect with them. I was afraid of feeling embarrassed or inferior, because my family's problems—including the fact that we were now dealing with a huge debt—were out in the open and rumors were spreading. I was scared of what my friends thought, or of finding out that they just didn't care. I felt like I needed something to disguise my feelings and put me in a position to hang out with my friends, something I could build on. I wasn't very interested in playing basketball. However, I saw that my buddies were excited about trying out for the team, and I figured it would be fun and that would give me the chance to re-establish some friendships by being part of the gang.

The idea sounded good. However, I forgot to recognize my emotional state at the time. I was in no frame of mind to play basketball. I was barely showing up to give fifty percent when I played hockey. Emotionally, I was a wreck, burdened with fatigue from the drain of my family life and the fact that I was finding it very difficult to sleep most nights. My self-confidence and self-esteem had become non-existent, and I felt like a complete failure. My normal, regular teenage life had increasingly amplified into a series of catastrophes. I was bottling up my feelings, making bad choice after bad choice, pushing people away instead of accepting or asking for support from anyone. My plan backfired as my situation became worse, because I didn't realize at the time that what I really needed was to reconnect with myself. I got to learn that lesson the hard way.

I went to basketball try-outs with my friends, and I made the team. In the beginning, things started out well; I was having fun and enjoying the camaraderie. However, something was missing. I was still torn, unable to re-establish my friendships the way I had planned. I wanted to know that my friends sincerely cared. It felt awkward, because I couldn't just come right out and talk to them about it. I was looking for signs to prove to me that they cared, but I never found any, because I couldn't figure out that I was still pushing people away with my attitude the way it was. As time went on, the only thing that was moving forward for me was my identity crisis. This started to affect my basketball performance, and things really went spinning out of control. Let's just say I was a much better hockey player than I was a basketball player. I found comfort in my attitude of, "What's the use?"

Needless to say, basketball wasn't going very well. I didn't see much action on the court. My coach cared about winning, and the only contribution he seemed to want from me was to keep the bench warm. All of sudden, before I knew what was going on, I was on the other side of the pendulum, in unknown territory. In hockey, I had been the player that the coach and team would count on to score the goal, the captain of the team—and now I felt like all I did was disappoint. I could see that my coach and teammates were disappointed with my lack of effort and ability on the basketball court, and I began to fall into a pit of self-pity, hating life.

I felt like my life was a big game of dominoes, and when my parents divorced, that knocked down the first piece. It threw me into a race against the chain as I tried to stop the pieces from falling and they continued to get knocked over, one by one. Next in line, my school grades dropped and my relationship with my girlfriend fell apart. Eventually, I just wanted to stop the race and give up, letting the pieces fall where they may.

I desperately wanted someone to care about me, someone to walk up and push me hard enough that I wouldn't push away, and I could just let it all out. However, I seemed to be winning the push contests. I was so entangled in a mess of deep emotions, being pulled in so many directions, that I couldn't see through my clouded thoughts and realize the person who I really wanted to care about me was *me*.

I needed to find my little spark of courage and pull myself back out of the hole I was falling into. This took two heartbreaking events, which happened back to back as I played basketball.

The first incident took place in our fifth regular-season game. I intercepted a pass from the opposing team, snatching the ball at center court. I was wide open on a clear breakaway, racing to the basket for a routine lay-up. I stumbled over my feet as I made my jump, sending the ball straight up into the air and missing the basket entirely. Imagine the laughter. Embarrassed, I took the ribbing I knew was coming, because I felt like it was an honest enough mistake. But as I walked back to the bench after a player change, I heard a comment that ripped my heart from my chest. Lionel, one of the parents, who happened to be an acquaintance of my mom and dad, yelled from the stands, "Craig, what would your dad say if he saw you do that?" That sunk me! I was ashamed to even give a thought to what my dad would think. He was extremely proud of my hockey abilities, and having Dad proud of me meant everything to me. I will never forget the sinking feeling I had when Lionel brought my dad's opinion into the picture. I cringed to myself as I thought maybe Lionel was right, and there really was no longer a reason for my dad to be proud of me. I fell farther down into the depths of fear and insecurity, and my self-confidence was blasted into tiny little pieces.

The second event occurred at our next home game, which was held in our school gymnasium. The gym was filled with students, fans, friends—and my girlfriend, Elizabeth. It was the first and only game that Elizabeth came to watch. I was so nervous and embarrassed. I hadn't told her anything about what was going on with me regarding basketball or my feeling that I had lost my friends. Elizabeth had come to my hockey games before, and she would sit proudly in the stands as she watched me play. I wanted to keep it that way; I did not want her at this basketball game, watching me make a fool out of myself on the court. In fact, I had specifically requested that she not come to the game, which erupted into us having a huge fight. She had stormed off, leaving me wondering if she would actually show up.

My eyes were glued to the stands as I searched for her throughout the warm-ups and the start of the game. I felt somewhat relieved that she apparently wasn't coming, but I also felt guilty about asking her not to. What right did I have to do that just because I was scared to tell her the truth about my basketball abilities? Ashamed, I rationalized my motives because I didn't think she would like me if I wasn't one of the best players. Things between us were hard enough at the time and I was scared to lose her. Then, about two minutes into the game, my heart began to race as I noticed the far door of the gymnasium open. It was Elizabeth! She was with one of her friends, Christy Lynn. My muscles began to tense and I tried not to hyperventilate. My butt felt paralyzed to the bench. Inside, I was shouting to myself, *Oh God, can this get any worse?!*

I sat on the bench for the entire first half. Our team was winning, the fans were cheering, and the coach was giving the team a pep talk to keep up the good play. I tried not to look over at Elizabeth. I was sure she would see my embarrassment. I was trying to think of what injury I should tell her I had, as I prayed that the coach wouldn't send me in to play.

The game continued until there were only two minutes left. We had a commanding lead when Mason, one of my teammates, leaned over to me and asked, "Have you played yet, Craig?" In a low whisper, signalling to Mason to be quiet, I said, "No," hoping the coach wasn't listening. However, as I turned my head, I noticed that he had indeed heard us. Anxiety consumed my body, and I thought to myself, *Oh no, the coach is going to put me in.* I stared at the score clock, watching the time tick down and feeling embarrassed at the idea of being sent on now, when we were winning and there was less than a minute left.

Unfortunately I made eye contact with the coach. He looked at me, then at the clock, then at me again—and began writing on his notepad. A moment later, I heard him yell, "Craig, Tim, Steve, get ready!" Agony gripped me as I prayed the whistle wouldn't blow. I was begging the seconds to tick off the clock, but they were moving more slowly than the days of January. The whistle sounded, just in time for a player change. As I walked onto the court, I looked up in the stands at Elizabeth. Then someone, mocking me, shouted over to her, "Craig's playing a great game, hey Elizabeth!" The whole gymnasium must have heard! I know Elizabeth did. My knees were wobbling, and I just wanted to walk off and go home. Instead, I ran down the court as a teammate passed me the ball. Gripping it in my hands, I dribbled and quickly passed it away to another teammate. He had just enough time to make some fancy moves, run the time off the clock, and put the ball up for a basket. Then the horn blew and the game was over.

As the fans cheered and congratulated our team on the win, I stood at center court, looking at Elizabeth and feeling ready to give up. I knew I wasn't the person she once knew, and I felt like I had just disappointed her. I had the gym door in my sights and was going to make a break for it when I saw Elizabeth running towards me. Frozen in embarrassment, I didn't know what to say or do. All I could do was stand there and take whatever she was going to say. To my surprise, she said nothing, but instead grabbed my hands and kissed me. Then she gently whispered in my ear, "Craig, I think you are great! Let's go home." I was shocked! How could I be great? Even in my weakest moment, someone thought I was great. Elizabeth never knew what her words did to me in that moment, but because she saw more in me than I did, I realized it was okay to be me. I didn't have to be great at basketball or a superstar hockey player, and I didn't have to have money or a happy home life in order to be worth something. I could simply be myself. That realization ignited a spark within me.

I knew I had to do something. I knew I needed to change how my life was going. I wanted to be the person I knew was inside me. That night, I listened to my heart and searched my soul for the strength I needed to start liking myself again. I made the decision to move on with life and face some of my fears with my friends.

Mom had told me when my parents divorced that one of the reasons she had to leave was because she needed her own identity. She didn't want to give up on herself. That night, as I stood on the basketball court, I realized I didn't want to give up on myself either. Though I still feel torn about Mom's reason, I could now understand her decision.

I felt invigorated by my decision. A new feeling of life awakened inside me. I felt stronger and more courageous. So what if I'm not the best basketball player? I was still good at some things and didn't need to be good at everything. We all have differences and unique talents. When my friends would tease me about my basketball abilities, I always replied, "When you're ready to lace up the skates and play some hockey, then we'll talk," knowing that some of them didn't know how to skate. Our differences make us who we are, and they make us special and worthwhile!

God was about to test my courage. I planned to talk to my coach at the next practice about how I felt I was letting the team down because of my attitude and lack of effort. I wanted to tell him I had decided to move on in order to sort some things out, and that I was quitting the team. It was there that I was tested. Before practice, the coach called a meeting to discuss some issues. I don't remember exactly what was said, but I do remember that at the end of the lecture, he mentioned that some players had been sitting on the bench because they were not showing enough drive, and he wanted that to improve. That was fine, until he pointed his finger at me by stating my name specifically in front of the whole team. Emotions revved inside of me—anger, guilt, insecurity, embarrassment, self-pity, and despair.

Although it seems all backwards, this was my test. I needed to stand strong in my decision. I was still great. I could not let my emotions get the best of me and suck me back into my tangled mess. I needed to be strong, so I asked to talk to my coach after everyone left to change. This was the moment when my spark began to create a fire. No more excuses about the divorce, or about my self-esteem. I went into his office, handed in my uniform, and told him I needed to move on. He asked why, and all I could tell him was that I needed to. It felt like a weight was lifted off my back. I took back my vulnerability, and I was going to start gaining my confidence back.

I found courage when I took control of my life. I needed to stand up for myself. It seems ironic that handing in my uniform was my answer, because I believe very strongly in perseverance, but basketball wasn't what was true for me. The truth was that I didn't want to play basketball. I simply wanted to reconnect with my friends. After I quit, I found courage to be myself and open up more freely with friends, which helped strengthen true friendships. Interestingly, some of my friends changed. I grew closer to people who I could relate to through more meaningful conversations, rather than simply because we were sports or party buddies. It felt good to recognize that I didn't have to justify myself to anyone.

It's amazing how life tests your will and shows you your victories in subtle ways when you least expect it. It was the next year and I was in Phys Ed class. My teacher that year, who had been my basketball coach the previous year, had us playing, of all things, basketball. The class had come to an end and we were cleaning up the basketballs, tossing them into the storage bin. In fun, I grabbed a basketball and bolted down the court, dribbling. I stopped and spun around, jumping in the air and shooting from outside the three-point line. I could hear the net go *swish* as the ball went into the basket without hitting the rim. I heard my teacher say, impressed, "Wow, Craig! You must have been practicing over the summer!" I paused for a minute, smiling at him as I turned around and said, "No, I just feel better." I can still see the bewildered look on his face, and I think we both saw more in me in that one moment than in the whole year before.

Building Self-Confidence

Realizing I was still okay as a person despite all the changes in my life was a turning point for me. I started to rebuild my confidence instead of wallowing in self-pity. I realized through my basketball experience that I had very low self-esteem and had lost my confidence. It hadn't always been that way. In fact, I had always been a strong, confident person. However, riding the emotional roller coaster of divorce is bound to shake you up and leave you searching your soul. I can guarantee that. When dealing and coping with the delicate matters of the heart that divorce brings, it's extraordinarily difficult to keep perspective. It takes immense inner strength. Building confidence becomes a fundamental part in accessing this strength in order to build a healthy future.

Somewhere along my journey, I had allowed myself to believe I wasn't worth anything anymore! I needed to make some changes in my life, my attitude, and my beliefs. The first step was to take ownership of my feelings, and this launched me in pursuit of bringing myself back to life.

To build my confidence back up, I decided it was necessary for me to try some new things. First, I was going to start to be honest with myself about who I was and what I was feeling. I wouldn't blame anyone else for my problems. I would try being open-minded to new ideas that came my way. Most importantly, I would try to love myself again by pointing out my small successes along the way. Step one: Take back control of my life. Step two: Take some time for myself to examine my true feelings, stop burying them inside, and face my fears. Step three: Ask for help when I need it and express my thanks and appreciation to those who help me.

With my steps in mind, I wrote a list of things I wanted to focus on as I continued my search for confidence and truth. I still follow this list:

- Remember how to dream again.
- Ask myself what I am really feeling in moments of pain or negative emotion, and determine how I could better the situation.
- Work on projects that are important to me.
- Set goals.

- Look for the lessons in the mistakes I have made and will continue to make.
- Stop dwelling on the past.
- Believe I can accomplish what I want in life, and that I deserve it because of what I can offer in return.
- Re-evaluate my priorities.
- Decide what is truly important and work towards it.
- Do not allow others to bring me down.
- Stay true to my dreams and never give up.
- Take some risks and trust my abilities.
- Acknowledge my successes, regardless of how little they are.
- Encourage others to pursue their talents and dreams.

Following my list has become a lifelong journey. Creating it helped me focus on myself and my future. It provided a positive influence on building my confidence and self-image, as opposed to the outside circumstances and garbage that had been influencing my choices prior to that. Building self-confidence really is a never-ending task. I need to consistently stay in touch with my inner strength.

Whenever I feel down, lost, beaten, or ready to quit, I remember to never give up on what I truly want. I reaffirm my list of goals and dreams and trust in my instincts, putting it up to God to lead the way.

As a side note, I have learned a cool strategy for working on building self-confidence. It was taught to me by one of my mentors, Bill Phillips. He suggests that it is important to acknowledge your little successes in order to get to the big ones. Each day, write down five things that you need to do or want to accomplish, no matter how small they may seem. The purpose is to congratulate yourself on your successes at the end of each day. This will help keep you focused as you work towards your bigger goals and dreams.

Improving self-confidence takes work and courage. It is a building block for our future and our choices. As human beings, regardless of what we do, we will have successes and failures. We can't always be perfect, but we can choose to never give up on ourselves. I have developed a belief that we all can achieve what we truly desire in life as long as we put our minds to it, focus, and align our self-image. We must pursue our purpose, simply by believing that we can do it!

The Impact of the Divorce On My Own Relationships

The divorce had a gigantic impact on my personal love relationships. As much as it affected me emotionally, it snowballed into the lives of others, because I was no longer able to trust. At fifteen, I had only just begun to learn about love when my parents split up. My behavior was influenced by the confusion I experienced during the chaotic times. I had all kinds of distorted thoughts and insecurities, and as a result, I displayed much inappropriate behavior with girlfriends. Not only did I have to rebuild confidence and trust in myself, I also had to learn how to find and use my strength to work on my relationships.

For many years, I hung on to these love and trust issues in order to protect myself from being hurt. More importantly, I didn't want to hurt anyone else. I felt torn. Deep down, I wanted someone to love me, but I couldn't bring myself to believe in love. I concluded that it didn't really exist—that there was no such thing as true love.

As my relationships developed, I found it extremely difficult to talk about the divorce with girlfriends. I felt like I couldn't let them know what was going on inside of me. Instead, I let my feelings erupt into fear about a girlfriend cheating or the relationship growing apart. I asked endless inappropriate questions and became very controlling, because I didn't want any surprises. I should have been honest and asked for patience and understanding, but I was too embarrassed, and I didn't want anyone to take pity on me. I would never let my guard down long enough to find out if I could trust a girl, or if she would understand. With the guilt I felt about my actions, I felt like I didn't deserve to be loved, and that I didn't have the ability to make a relationship work.

I discovered what was really happening and why I was consistently running away from women. I couldn't accept love from anyone else because for a long time, I no longer loved myself. If I didn't feel that I was good enough, how could I believe anyone else would? I chose to push love away until my girlfriends didn't want me anymore. The truth was that I didn't want to push them away; I wanted to be reassured. I wanted them to constantly prove to me that they loved me. In doing so, I never had to risk my heart being broken. I couldn't bear to take the kind of pain I would feel if I gave my heart to someone, only to lose her in the end. I spent more time finding fault in everything and everyone, rather than seeking what I really wanted: to be loved.

This was exactly what I did to Elizabeth when I broke up with her about ten months after my parents divorced. It was our first big breakup. Things were going very well between us when I phoned her that fateful day to share the news that my parents were splitting up. That changed our relationship. After the divorce, because I was going through extreme emotional turmoil, there was unbelievable tension between us. We were both confused about why my parents had divorced. As much as Elizabeth tried to help me through this hard time, I felt it was too much for me to ask, and too much for her to have to bear. There were so many things I wanted her to understand, and I simply felt that she couldn't. It turned our young, fun, puppy-love romance into a serious, conflict-ridden, intense relationship.

Elizabeth had some turmoil to deal with in her own life, and I wasn't much help to her because I was so consumed by my feelings. I began to dominate conversations, analyzing every little detail and looking for signs that she cared about me. I started to get jealous and expected her to read my mind and know exactly what I needed. She supported me and listened. I was in a crisis, and I couldn't help feeling that I was deeply hurting her as well. I felt extremely guilty because I was so much in need of her, and yet I couldn't be there for her. I made an impulse decision when it felt like it was too much, and I ran away. I thought it wasn't fair to Elizabeth to involve her in my pain, and I felt she deserved better than that.

Elizabeth had phoned me and I was really feeling down that day. I was depressed about the mess of a person I had become, and embarrassed about how I had been treating her. I knew I was hurting her and I didn't want to anymore, but I also knew I was far from getting a grip on myself. She kept asking me what was wrong, and I kept saying it was nothing and that I didn't want to talk about it. Elizabeth's voice started to crackle, and out of nowhere, she asked me, "Craig, do you want to break up with me?" I had never even considered breaking up with her before that moment, and didn't want to. However, for some reason, I felt like it was my only answer to stop the pain and guilt, and to let her find happiness with someone else. I no longer felt good enough. Before I had a chance to think, I said softly, "Yes." The phone went silent and before I had a chance to explain anything, she hung up on me. I thought I was looking out for her and protecting her, but in reality, I was scared and needed time to sort out my problems.

By breaking it off like I did, I ended up hurting Elizabeth more than I ever could have by accepting her help, love, and compassion. It wasn't fair for me to make a decision that really should have been hers. I should have been honest with her and told her I needed time to deal with all the confusion and emotions the divorce brought. The guilt I felt about dragging her into my problems was just way too much for me to handle, and I never gave her the chance to decide if she wanted it. I didn't want to break up with her; I simply thought it was the right thing to do. After some time, I realized what I had done was wrong, but it was too late. The damage was done, and I had hurt and scarred both of us deeply. Eventually, we did get back together and found some happiness for a time. However, with the pain of unresolved issues that we didn't know how to fix, Elizabeth and I found we needed to walk our own paths. We again went our separate ways.

As time went on, I continued to push people away and avoided talking about my issues and true feelings. It became a pattern, and I would always lose out in the end. My relationships started out fun and vibrant, full of energy and romance—but as soon as I saw the first sign that it was becoming closer and more intimate, my emotions would spin out of control. Deep-seated pain would churn in the bottom of my stomach, and my attitude would do a 180. The caution flag would wave in front of my face, which was my cue to run out the back door before I got myself into a potentially explosive or hurtful situation. I always had this hidden fear of challenging fate, as I believed my girlfriends would leave me in the end anyway. I felt as though as soon as I allowed myself to be vulnerable enough to fall in love, it would somehow be ripped away from me.

My behavior changed. I became a different person, falling into jealous rages and questioning every little thing. I was constantly searching for lies, finding fault, and often intentionally hurting my partners in order to drive away the possibility of being hurt myself. Then the guilt would flood my heart, because I knew what I was doing was wrong. I couldn't understand how to control it. It was totally unfair to anyone I had a relationship with, and in the end, all I ever did was hurt the people I cared about.

Part of my mess, of course, was my immaturity as an adolescent. I was just learning about matters of the heart, which only magnified the confusion. The pain of the divorce seriously affected my ability to love unconditionally. No matter how much I knew it was wrong, and no matter what harm it caused others or myself, I couldn't trust anyone. I battled with myself unconsciously, sabotaging relationships by putting conditions on my love interests, stating things like, "If you loved me, you wouldn't talk to your friend John on the phone anymore," or "You should make me the first priority in your life so I know you love me." I was making mistake after mistake. I became especially paranoid when something happened in my relationship that was similar to the reasons my parents divorced. In those moments, I became cold and callous, and without a shadow of a doubt, the relationship was doomed!

I was in rough shape when it came to relationships. I decided that it would be best for me to stay single for awhile—to sort out my feelings until I was ready to make a real, honest effort. For a long time, it seemed I would be single for the rest of my life and just have fun—although deep in my heart, I always knew I wanted a loving wife and family. I almost hated myself for wanting that.

After a couple years of trying to deny to myself that I wanted to get married, I could no longer do that. This realization was like a first step towards marriage. I was beginning to feel more ready to risk being loved and to try to start actually trusting someone. I knew I had to do it if I ever wanted love in my life. It was like that old saying that I kept telling myself to build up my courage: "It is better to have loved and lost than never to have loved at all."

When I met Trina, the woman who would become my wife, my entire life came unglued. She had a profound effect on me and challenged me to look at myself in the mirror and love the person I saw—because she did. Trina had a way of expressing her love to me, and I knew she saw more inside of me than I did. Our relationship started out wonderfully, but as it progressed, I came to the point where I felt those issues rumbling through my mind, which was my cue to call it quits. However, no matter how much I wanted to run away, I couldn't. Every time I tried to end it, I bit my tongue and felt her words in my heart. I had a hard time trusting her. However, when I questioned Trina or found fault, she would never give up. She also never took any garbage from me, always asking me to love her for who she was, as she did for me.

Slowly, with Trina's help, I chose to stand up to myself and face my demons. I decided to risk my heart because I was falling in love. Because of her incredible patience and our shared desire to understand each other, I couldn't let go of her. I couldn't imagine not having her in my life. At the same time, it wasn't easy. I would be lying if

I said our relationship didn't get out of control and crazy at times. For both of us, it became the ultimate roller-coaster ride—until the day I finally decided to ask her to marry me. It wasn't an easy road for us. I'm amazed and deeply thankful that she hung in there with me through our good and bad times. Through it all, we learned how to periodically reconnect with each other, and we continue to fall in love as we go along.

As I write this book today, I owe much gratitude to the people I shared relationships with. A special thanks to Elizabeth, who stood beside me through some of my weakest moments at the time of the divorce. It is because of the lives that touched mine, and the lessons I learned from them, that I can now open my heart to Trina and risk being in love.

It took me a long time and an enormous amount of strength to recognize what I was missing and realize what I was doing to myself. Ironically, as much as I chose to inflict negative consequences on my relationship because of the issues that scared me so much, the divorce also forced me to examine my feelings and search for answers so that Trina and I could create a loving relationship. I strongly believe that the divorce, despite the pain and loss it brought, contributed to my ability to find true love with Trina. If the divorce hadn't happened, I don't think I would have found it so important to dig deep into my soul and make decisions about the type of loving family I wanted. I wouldn't have learned the things I did about myself, and I wouldn't have understood how important it is to love and accept yourself before you can love another completely and unconditionally.

Our Choices Control Our Future

Through the divorce, I found that the traumatic experiences I had to endure made me start to ask big questions about my life. I recognized that I needed great courage to determine my future and move forward towards my aspirations.

I recall one instance where I was sitting in my thinking chair, feeling depressed—like I just couldn't handle my life anymore. I had just lost one of my closest friends in a tragic accident, and I again found myself plagued by that dreaded question: Why? Why did someone so young have to die? There was no answer, just as there hadn't been with my parents' divorce. It wasn't fair, and again, I had no control. As I sat there, overcome by so many mixed emotions, one in particular stood out. I was completely fed up with myself about how I had allowed the pain of my parents' divorce to become an excuse for the rest of my life. I felt I had lost so many things that were dear to me, and that I would never again find happiness, someone to love, or anything meaningful in my life. I spent the rest of the night in my thinking chair, consumed by self-pity.

I started thinking about my past experiences, my parents' divorce, giving up my hockey dream, and giving up on myself. I wondered how I had ended up sitting there, feeling sorry for myself and wishing I still had all the things I had lost.

I asked myself a question that night: "Craig, how much longer do you really want to continue living in self-pity, pain, and hate, blaming the world for your troubles?" I began to contemplate what I wanted to do with my life, who I was, who I really wanted to become, and what I wanted to accomplish. Emotionally, spiritually, economically, socially, and physically, I had choices to make. Even in my sorrow, somewhere deep inside I knew I wanted to make my life better. I didn't know how; I just knew I wanted more. As I sat there, I told myself, "Despite everything—my mistakes, my hardships, and my pain —before I die, I want to do something important and be someone special in this world. I want to do incredible things in my life and leave a legacy of contributions and accomplishments that I will be remembered for." At that moment, I knew I had something to say, something I wanted to tell the world—I just didn't yet know what it was.

I realized that even though life had brought me many unfair, agonizing, uncontrollable circumstances, I still had choices. I had the opportunity to redesign and create the rest of my life. I didn't have to live under these circumstances, continually making excuses. We are responsible for our actions and reactions; they are all we can control. I believe we are all born into this world as equals, and we all eventually die. How we deal with and adapt to the bad and good in the middle is up to us. It's ultimately our choice in the end.

Divorce, for the most part, is a negative experience, but it can have some positive outcomes. One of the most positive effects the divorce had on me was that I found the strength to face my fears. The more I confronted my fears, the more I began to triumph over my issues. I then felt successful, which created a more positive attitude in me. It helped me realize that when you really want something in life, you should wholeheartedly pursue it. Break through your fears and go for it!

Believe In Yourself

I was eighteen years old when a friend of the family introduced Dad to a home-based business opportunity with a new product line of perfume and cologne. Money was a major priority for me at that time because of the financial crisis I was in, so I was eager to find a way to earn more. I happened to overhear their conversation and thought the business might be a good opportunity for me as well. It was affordable for a guy with no money, it boasted strong income potential, and I didn't need any experience—just ambition, drive, and motivation. I asked Dad if I too could get involved, in an attempt to take a positive approach and change my life for the better. He said yes, so I launched my first business venture—selling perfume and cologne.

Some time later, I was at a business conference that the company was hosting. I really didn't want to be there, because it was expensive and my business was taking somewhat of a downturn. (I had run out of Grandma's friends to sell to!) However, in an attempt to revive the business and rekindle my spark of motivation, I agreed to go. I'm very glad I did, because it was there that I met one of my mentors, Mark Victor Hansen, who opened me up to the possibilities in life and the importance of believing in yourself.

Hansen was the guest speaker. He walked onto the stage, poised and polished, and caught me completely off guard as he began his talk. He was charismatic, energetic, and full of life and positive emotion. He was obviously very well-read and successful. He was what I wanted to be like, doing what I wanted to do—inspire others about their potential. He had powerful messages, and I listened to everything he had to say. I could relate to so many things. It really inspired me to see someone who had come through so much in his life develop the confidence to turn things around and create his future the way he wanted it to be. As I sat, absorbed by his words, I could feel my body ease and release positive emotions, because his ideas were grabbing hold of me, making sense to me. I had been storing up so much pain and trying so hard to turn hardships into great triumphs. As Hansen talked, I began to identify my potential. I realized I needed to believe in myself, trust my instincts, and know that I had something to contribute to the world.

I connected strongly with his speech, especially when it came to feelings about the heart, family, and love. I could address my issues more clearly when I heard others' stories and what they went through. I didn't feel so alone anymore.

The life principles Hansen was sharing were powerful, practical tools I could use and build on. These were lessons and insights he had learned through his experiences. His stories got me thinking about the decisions I needed to make about what I wanted to do and become in my life. I had been struggling through the divorce battle for a few years, and it was incredibly refreshing to listen to someone with such a positive spirit for life. He set a strong example of believing in yourself, having a dream, setting goals, and actually accomplishing those goals. He could certainly motivate! I felt desires igniting in me as he told us to write down some goals that we wanted to accomplish and dreams that we aspired to. I felt like they were right in front of me; I could just reach out and grab them! It felt good to be able to dream again. It had been a long time since I had thought about a dream.

Hansen said, "Goal setting is goal getting," and that setting goals is the first step to believing in yourself, no matter what anyone else says. My parents and playing hockey had taught me the importance of setting goals and following a plan. But somehow during the divorce, I had forgotten about all of that, and I was eager to find it again.

I began writing away, and my mind became more clear and focused. I felt like I was really taking control of my life, and it was easy. I listened to what was in my heart and forgot about all the reasons why I believed I couldn't do certain things or pursue my dreams. While I was doing this, I remembered what my grandma had taught me a few years back. She said that when she is faced with difficult choices, she trusts her instincts. She explained, "Every time I have followed my gut feeling, it hasn't steered me wrong, but when I went against it, most times things didn't work out." As I wrote down some of my goals, I could literally feel my gut instincts roaring, *Yes!* I knew the direction I should take and what I wanted to do with the rest of my life. It all began to unfold before my eyes.

If we listen to our hearts, we will find that life is waiting for us to grab hold of it. We should start today and never, ever give up on our dreams. If we find the lessons in our mistakes and hardships, they will keep us on track during our pursuit.

I would like to share some of my dreams with you in the hopes that they might help stimulate your thoughts and ignite some of your desires. I believe we all need to dream and create goals as a working blueprint toward achieving our dream.

1. Marry the woman of my dreams—very loving and caring, patient, great motherhood aspirations, honest, ambitious, gorgeous, great sense of humor, shares my ideals, and loves to have fun. Have two to four beautiful children and a loving family.

2. Become an inspiring, motivating, and entertaining speaker.

3. Write a book and become a best-selling author.

4. Write a movie screenplay.

5. Write a hit song and have Garth Brooks sing it.

6. Help my mom, dad, and brother pursue one of their dreams.

7. Live healthy and in excellent physical condition.

8. Own my own corporation and hold shares in other business interests.

9. Go to the Academy Awards.

10. Win a business award.

11. Bench-press 400 pounds to beat my dad's record of 390.

12. Build my family dream house on ten acres of land and include a waterslide from my bedroom to an indoor pool. (A childhood dream that I am still holding onto!)

13. Swim with the dolphins with my wife and children.

14. Become a spokesperson for a cause I believe in.

15. Inspire one person each year to become a writer or a speaker.

16. Earn my black belt in a martial art.

It may take many years before these dreams become reality, and I might not achieve some of them at all. However, the fun and the passion that I feel come from the journey of pursuing them. The secret is to persevere and be consistent and continually focused on moving towards your dreams by setting attainable goals. I find that writing them down helps initiate your journey, provides direction, and sets your intention. The rest is up to you, through your belief in yourself and commitment to never give up on yourself—because you're worth it.

Many years ago, as I walked the journey through my parents' divorce, I found a poem that helped me make it through some sleepless nights. I read it now and then when I feel my belief being shaken and my strength slipping away. It gives me the boost I need, keeping me focused. I apologize that I don't know who wrote it, but I would like to share it with you. It always inspires me and brings out my inner strength.

I'm Special

In the entire world, there is nobody like me. Since the beginning of time, there has never been another person like me. Nobody has my smile. Nobody has my eyes, my nose, my hair, my hands, and my voice.

I'm special.

In all of time there has been no one who laughs like me, no one who cries like me. And what makes me laugh and cry will never provoke identical laughter and tears from anybody else, ever.

I'm the only one in creation who has my set of abilities. Oh, there will always be somebody who is better at one of the things I'm good at, but no one in all the universe can reach the quality of my combination of talents, ideas, abilities, and feelings.

Through all of eternity no one will ever look, talk, walk, think, or do like me. I'm special; I'm rare.

And as in all rarity, there is great value. Because of my great rare value, I need not attempt to imitate others. I will accept—yes, celebrate—my differences.

I'm special.

And I'm beginning to realize it's no accident that I'm special. I'm beginning to see that God made me special for a very special purpose.

He must have a job for me that no one else can do as well. Out of all the billions of applicants, only one is qualified, only one has the right combination of what it takes.

That one is me.

Because ... I'm special!

~Author Unknown

CHAPTER SEVEN
New Relationships

*"When my parents divorced, my heart felt like a pincush-
ion and my mind was closed to reason. Through the
friendships that I built along the way, I was able to heal
my broken heart and face my fear of abandonment. In
time, the support I received taught me the importance of
acceptance and love, and the value of a hug!"*

~Kate Rogers

In the beginning, my parents starting to date others reminded me
of the movie "Jaws." Just when I thought it was safe to let my guard
down and take a breath, *Crunch!* The dating shark attacked and a
new person was on the arm of Mom or Dad, adding yet another element to my journey as their new relationships developed.

I was overcome by the most awkward feeling I had ever felt as my
parents began to date. It was disturbing; it felt so wrong and
unorthodox that Mom and Dad were seeing other people. I had no
idea how to deal with the foreign feelings I was experiencing, and I
didn't know whether to like or hate the people my parents dated.
What if I didn't like them? Was I supposed to pretend that I did? And
what if I did like them? Would I be betraying Mom or Dad? I would
question the motives of my parents' companions, and I found it
extremely difficult to accept, especially because I understood what
my parents were really doing. They were human too, but the mere
idea of my Mom or Dad having sex with other people sent chills
down my spine. It put too many awful pictures and worries into my
head—fear of all kinds of things, such as new brothers and sisters

competing for time and attention, my parents not protecting themselves from the risks of disease, and the idea of my parents remarrying, meaning I would have a new stepparent trying to take the place of my mom or dad. The potential of new issues, problems, and dilemmas was enormous and for the most part, out of my control.

I never knew when Mom or Dad would bring someone new into their life and what that would bring. Sometimes they brought different beliefs, different cultural backgrounds, different morals and ethics, religious differences, undesirable histories, and baggage—all of which added to the stress. It amplified the tension between all of us who were involved, causing more and more problems. However, through these experiences, I also learned that each situation that arises is unique. Many times, my parents' boyfriends and girlfriends brought forward positive qualities, and I saw that there was potential for them to create a healthy relationship with Mom or Dad. This is a situation that I hope one day will happen. Although I don't think I will ever like my parents dating, it is a reality that I have to accept. All I can do is hope that they make good choices.

By far, the toughest part for me to deal with was the new private life that formed for both Mom and Dad. It is something I will always have to accept, but even today, I still don't want to have to. My parents' dating was a part of their individual lives, and not a part of mine. It was uncomfortable for me to talk to them about their boyfriends and girlfriends, and that separated us further. When my parents were married, they could share some of their loving moments with Wes and me as they hugged and kissed each other. However, I didn't want to have any part of that as they dated; I wasn't interested in witnessing it or hearing about it. Other things in their lives became more important to them, and their time became divided between what we did together and what they did separately.

I have always hated having to share my parents' time and constantly compromise as they became involved in romances, emotional angst, other people's schedules, and other people's children's schedules. They had to work around all of these things in order to find the time to fit me in. Although it wasn't like I wanted to spend all of my time with my parents, I still wanted to feel involved in their lives and important to them. The sheer fact that there were so many more variables to consider before we could plan to do anything, especially on holidays, left me frustrated. I felt like their whole priority structure had collapsed, and it seemed that my needs took a back seat to others'. It was disheartening trying to come up with compromises that best fit everyone all of the time. This often left me filled with resentment, as most times I ended up giving in to my parents' requests of involving their boyfriend or girlfriend in our activities or events together. Mainly because I felt it was the only way I would get a chance to see Mom or Dad, and I didn't want to be left out in the cold. I took what I could get, especially at Christmas. It became easier to just throw my hands in the air, say, "Who cares," and forget about it, rather than to continually fight.

Too many new relationships formed for me when my parents embraced their private lives. I now had a different relationship with Mom and Dad individually, a new relationship with each parent and his/her new partner together, an individual relationship with each of these boyfriends and girlfriends, and at times, new relationships with their children. It seemed to go on and on. It was so overwhelming, and most times I didn't have the energy to even keep up, let alone think about it.

I resented the fact that it felt like my parents were forcing people on Wes and me, pressuring us to like them just because they wanted everyone to get along. It was hard because before the divorce, Wes and me were used to being my parents' biggest priority, and they were focused on our lives and our family. That all changed as it became very important for Mom and Dad to focus on their own individual needs. I was mad at them for it, and yet I couldn't say anything. When I did, I ended up feeling guilty for trying to take away any happiness they might find by asking them not to date.

The whole thing completely changed my relationship with my parents. I had a harder time seeing them as parents. I had begun my own experiences with dating, and this was almost at the same time that Mom and Dad entered the dating world. I felt like I was somehow sharing this part of my life with them, as though they were my buddies at high school and we were learning about relationships together. It was awkward because it altered my perception of my parents and what I really wanted from them. I wanted to feel like I could go to them when I was struggling with my own relationships, and they could offer expert advice along the way. It just wasn't that simple anymore, because with them being divorced, I could no longer trust their guidance. Somehow I developed this block in my relationships, trying not to do the things my parents had done, because ultimately their relationship had ended in divorce. A new twist entered into my relationship with Mom and Dad, and it became harder to see them as authority figures because I seemed to be offering as much advice to them as they were to me. Because of how awkward everything became, I found it worked better when I started to build a new relationship with my parents as friends, instead of the parent and child relationship.

First Reaction

My initial reaction to my parents' dating was to pretend it didn't bother me and find ways to avoid being around when they went out on dates. At first, I couldn't digest the whole idea; it was too much to handle. It was terrifying and embarrassing to ask about it, because I knew I didn't want to hear the things I was going to.

I did a good job of avoiding it up until the time that I started to notice Mom dating a guy named Dave on more of a regular basis. That brought too many concerns for me to ignore. My need to protect Mom became immense. I had to be absolutely certain that she was safe and there was no threat of any danger like physical or verbal abuse, disease, addiction problems, or even possible manipulation from Dave. I didn't know Dave's past history very well and I didn't know what his true motives were, not to mention my mom's. This was the first time I really wanted answers to my questions about her dating, and it launched me into a mini-crisis.

I remember when Mom first introduced me to Dave. I shook his hand and said, "Nice to meet you," but the only thought going through my head was, *Who in the heck is this joker? He can't hold a candle to Dad.* Launching my own internal investigation to determine if Dave was a good guy, I began to watch obsessively. I probed Mom for information here and there, but I could never ask her the important questions. So I acted like a spy, driving myself crazy as I tried to listen in on their conversations in order to determine Dave's past history, the possibility of a criminal record, reasons for his previous divorce, if they were intimate, and whether or not he had good intentions. I kept a keen eye on when and where Mom went out with Dave. I monitored the time she spent with him and found myself trying to make sense of what would happen.

Underneath, I knew my craziness came from the fear and guilt I felt about betraying Dad by liking Dave. I felt responsible for protecting my Dad's feelings, and as much as I wanted to protect Mom, I also wanted to find reasons why no one could ever be better than Dad. In addition, when Dave entered the picture, I felt threatened because it seemed that he would take my place, too. Dad wasn't the man of the house in Mom's life anymore, and as the oldest boy in the family, I felt I was to play that role. Although in my heart I know that no one could ever take the place of my mom or dad, I am still scared that someone may try.

For the most part, I have to admit that my parents are good judges of character. The people they date are usually nice and have positive qualities. However, I recall that sometimes Wes and I had a good laugh when we met some of their dates. I'm not trying to demean anyone by saying that; I think it was more of a way that Wes and me could connect with each other. Making a wisecrack or two seemed to help us deal with the awkwardness we felt.

Although I will never want my parents to be with anyone but each other, I also know in my heart that I don't want them to spend the rest of their lives alone. I want each of them to find happiness, comfort, and joy in a relationship. They deserve it just as much as we all do.

Dad Gets Serious

Through the turmoil we experienced, my dad and I grew closer than we had ever been before. As we continued to confront the issues between us, those extreme moments when we fought became calmer and less dramatic. We were able to get our thoughts out on the table and discuss solutions to make things better, working through them together. I felt good about how our relationship was developing into a strong friendship, and I was proud of how much we had come through. After the hardships we had dealt with during Dad's initial dating spurt, I became accustomed to his casual dating and for the most part, it felt harmless. It wasn't as important for him to invest all of his time in it, which left Wes and me higher in the priority chain. I liked it that way, because we all benefited. Dad could have fun and enjoy his life romantically, yet we still felt important to him. My mistake was that I thought it would stay that way.

When Dad fell for Julia, a bomb dropped on our relationship and everything we had built exploded. From the first time I met Julia, I sensed things were going to be different, and a strange, nervous sensation ran through my body. I could see something in Dad's eyes, and his tone of voice told me that Julia wasn't going to be like the other women he had dated. She seemed nice, but right away I felt threatened.

Dad completely changed and fell into a whole new life crisis of his own. He totally forgot about Wes and me. The interest he had in my life, my friends, doing things together, the disc jockey business, and simply being at home and joking around together—all of that disappeared. This left me with the responsibility of picking up the pieces, especially regarding our commitment to the business. Dad became a different person—serious and determined, like he was on a mission to win Julia over. I was lost at his behavior and became resentful towards both of them. I tried to rationalize the situation to myself, justifying Dad's behavior because I believed he needed time to figure out some relationship issues because of the divorce. However, when I found out that Julia had two kids and Dad was not only investing time with them but also spending money on them, that was too much for me. Wes and me needed his help financially, so he wasn't going to get any sympathy or understanding from me. I became enraged as it felt like I got dealt right out of my Dad's life.

Everything for Dad became about Julia. Even when we did talk, Dad spent most of his time defending her to me, justifying his relationship as I asked questions or protested what he was doing. He would get angry with me and bombard me with question after question, asking why I didn't like the situation. Eventually, I would just give in and agree with his position. I hated feeling like he was forcing Julia and her kids on me, when all I wanted was to feel that Dad and I still had some kind of relationship.

I remember sitting in the backyard one night, listening to the crackle of the bonfire and wondering what had happened to my dad. I wondered how suddenly everything could change so drastically. I wondered how Wes felt, seeing that he lived with Mom and probably rarely spoke to Dad anymore. I said a prayer that night in hopes that the situation would be temporary and that Dad would come around and start acting like himself again.

I couldn't completely understand his need to pursue Julia as aggressively as he did. He seemed willing to sacrifice so much. I knew Dad had many unresolved issues from the past, and it seemed he was trying to deal with them through this relationship. However, I didn't comprehend why it had to be the way it was, and when I asked, he just told me I wouldn't understand, which left me feeling like it was hopeless.

As time went on, their commitment grew stronger and things

started to get very ugly between Dad and me. When he started talking about marriage with Julia, it scared me to the point where I completely gave up on him. Right from day one, his relationship seemed to start off on the wrong foot with the rest of us. For instance, when Dad introduced Julia to our family members, she clashed with many of us, turning an already dangerous situation into a nightmare. No one was supportive, and all I can say is that things happened that brought the worst out in some people. I felt for Dad as other people came down on him hard, but it was difficult for me to be helpful because I couldn't let go of the anger or hurt I felt toward Dad for not listening to me. It became a trying time. Dad became so defensive, and he lost sight of the truth that he was neglecting our feelings. It felt like he was a walking time bomb.

I didn't know what to do about the situation as it brought me into territory I never wanted to be in. We had come a long way together to weather the divorce, and now it seemed like Dad was on his way to building a new family of his own. That hurt, but I knew I had to bring some peace back into our lives, as I felt extremely threatened that life with Dad would never be the same again. I had to come to some conclusions and find a way to be civil. All I could do was tell Dad how I felt. I couldn't control his decision to marry Julia. Therefore, I concluded that I would have to accept it. It was his choice. I decided I would honor his decision and support him as long as he understood that my relationship with Julia was mine and not his. That way, I could deal with issues I had with Julia without Dad's interference, and also deal with Dad without Julia's interference.

As difficult as the situation was and as hard as it was for Dad and me to find peace with each other, it taught me an important lesson about myself. I can't control other people; all I can control are my own choices. I learned how to deal with intense conflict and found I need only be responsible for my own feelings and actions. Life will bring difficult challenges and sometimes we are forced to accept things as they are in order to find peace for ourselves. As important as it is to me to have Dad involved in my life, I also realized it is equally as important for him to have someone he loves in his. Even though Julia didn't turn out to be the one, and they eventually broke up, I hope that one day Dad finds that perfect person to share his life and grow old with. When he does marry again, it will be the start of another journey for us.

Mom Announces Her Engagement

The phone rang early one afternoon and it was Mom, who said she was on her way over to my place with some big news. She didn't give a hint as to what the news was. Curious, I hung up the phone and waited impatiently. It caught me by surprise and I really had no idea what it could be. On the phone, Mom had sounded hesitant and yet excited. Perhaps, I hoped, she had won the lottery or was going to surprise Trina and me with an early wedding present! I yelled to Trina, "My mom just phoned and said she was on her way over with some big news." Trina walked into the living room, intrigued. We began to innocently ponder ideas back and forth, playing a guessing game for the next half-hour.

Seconds after the buzzer rang at our apartment, Trina blurted out, "I know what it is, Craig! Your mom is getting married!" A strange sensation swept through me, tying my stomach into knots as I allowed the possibility to hit me. Pretending to laugh at the remark, I said, "Very funny, Trina. It couldn't be. Mom has only been dating Sam for a short time and besides, I hardly know him." Trina just smiled as she said, "I don't know, Craig. I don't know." Before I could continue to defend my position, there was a knock at the door. Mom stood in the doorway with a peculiar look on her face, a worried and excited look. I knew she had something important to tell me, but she was obviously scared to. I became nervous, wondering if Trina could be right.

We made our way into the living room to sit down, and I watched my mom search for words as Trina smiled in anticipation. Mom took a deep breath and began to explain that she had some good news, but wasn't sure how I, in particular, was going to handle it. I started to brace myself, thinking this couldn't be good. Mom went on for a while nervously, beating around the bush, until both

Trina and I were sitting on the edge of our seats. Trina beat me to the punch and came right out and asked, "Are you getting married?" Mom hesitated and smiled nervously at Trina. Turning towards me, she said, "Yes, I am getting married." Trina jumped off the couch with cheers of excitement and congratulated Mom with a hug. My whole body felt like it had frozen to my chair. Sitting there, numb, I couldn't believe Trina was right. I didn't know what to say. In order not to create an even more awkward situation, I congratulated Mom and gave her a hug, wondering to myself how this could be. Dumbfounded, I asked, "When did this happen, Mom?" She answered, "The night before last." She continued to describe Sam's proposal, their future plans of a new house, and the wedding day.

I paced back and forth from the kitchen, trying to figure out what I actually thought, while Mom kept talking. Trina and I were to be married in a month, and here was my mom announcing that she would be getting married too. It felt unusual and threatening in many ways. I debated my concerns. Who was this Sam guy? I didn't know him very well and that scared me.

That was going to be my first mission: the Sam investigation. I started to ask Mom casual questions about Sam. As she talked more about him, I learned that he had three daughters, worked for a good company, and Mom obviously felt he treated her with respect. I decided to trust her judgment before I said anything. I didn't want to burden her with my feelings and have her miss out on happiness, especially with everything that had happened between Dad and me. I knew she wouldn't marry just anyone, and that she was a good judge of character. I still wanted to make sure she would be safe, but I decided to give it a chance before I let my emotions get the best of me.

I listened as Trina and Mom talked, adding the odd comment in order to appear involved in the conversation, until Mom noticed I had backed off. She said, "Craig, I want to let you know that if you have some issues with this, I'm open to discussing them with you and working them out." I didn't know what to say, but I appreciated her offer. In my heart, I was happy that Mom had found happiness. I didn't want her to be alone for the rest of her life, so even though I had concerns, I decided it was more important that I stand behind her. I said, "No, it's okay, Mom. I am happy for you and I will support you on it. I promise that if I have any serious concerns, I will let you know." Deep down, I know that part of me was also too scared to say anything out of fear of embarrassment—because it would mean I might have to admit I still had secret fantasies that my parents would somehow get back together. It seemed so childish. I kept my thoughts to myself and decided to trust that she was doing what she wanted. I wished her all the best.

In the end, it didn't work out for Sam and Mom and, after being engaged for close to a year, Mom called the wedding off. During the engagement, I did my best to support Mom, telling myself to trust her even when I noticed something I didn't like. It was her life, and since I wanted her to have a life with someone she could love, I let these issues go, as long as they didn't seem earth-shattering. Even though the relationship with Sam didn't last, I know one day Mom will marry someone who is right for her. Somehow, after their breakup, I felt that perhaps Mom's engagement wasn't really just about getting married. I believe it was also about her being able to tell me that someday, she might want to—and for me to understand that.

Extended Families

I haven't actually had to live with a true extended family, because my parents have yet to remarry. Therefore, I can't comment on exactly what it would be like. However, the experience that I do have comes from the days when I moved back in with Dad after he took a new job that allowed him to be home and eliminated travel from his agenda. He was renting an old acreage farmhouse at the time, and in order to save some money, he arranged for Ivy, a "woman friend" as he called her, and her fourteen-year-old daughter, Eve, to move in with us. Having grown up with only one brother, I found that living with Ivy and Eve was not only all new to me, but it also gave a whole new meaning to the term "family dynamics."

Adjusting to the new living arrangement started off more as a novelty, as everything was new and interesting. We were all very polite and conscious of each other's needs as we got to know one another. However, as time went on, awkward situations began to develop, creating a whole new world for me. As we began to learn to live with one another, I felt like I was getting a crash course on how to deal with people's boundaries, how to tolerate habits, and how to understand women's issues and behaviors.

The relationship my Dad had with Ivy was undetermined and they didn't make things clear, leaving Eve and I with many unanswered questions. That added stress because when I asked Dad about it, he sidestepped the issue, telling me they were friends and making the situation out to be something different than what it felt like. I never pushed it, because I figured what was the point? It would only make things more stressful and awkward than they already were. There was some comfort in keeping the situation a mystery, because it allowed me to avoid having to deal with issues I had about Dad and Ivy possibly becoming an item.

Ivy and Eve lived with us for over two years, and since I had never lived with a sister before, this posed many different difficulties and negotiations for me. For one, with only one bathroom in the house and about twenty minutes of hot water for showers in the morning, bathroom time became a never-ending dilemma. I was left with the short end of the stick many mornings as I left for school without a shower and the sound of hairdryers echoing through the house. Another major problem was the phone. Is it just me, or can teenage girls talk on the phone? Wow! Fortunately, Ivy put in a separate phone line for Eve, as otherwise it was going to become an impossible situation. I'm sure Ivy and Eve had complaints about some of my habits, too. I know I didn't make sharing the television an easy task.

The most difficult element I found was respecting each other's boundaries. Learning how to do that really set the tone for me in understanding what it would be like to experience living with a stepparent and new brothers or sisters. All of us have boundaries, a needed level of privacy, personal belongings we don't want touched, good and bad habits, and a need for our own space. Life with Ivy and

Eve became completely a trial-and-error situation. We never knew when one of us would be pushed too far and explode.

You really learn about people when you live with them—not to mention how much you learn about yourself. Communication and compromise become key components to finding the best solutions to dilemmas. However, sometimes it's just too hard and in the end, choices have to be made. Fortunately, we found ways to put some of our own needs aside in order to make it through without extreme fighting. It is never an easy task, but like many, we managed and became good friends. Every now and then, I think of Ivy and Eve and I miss some of the fun we had together. I hope they are well.

A few years ago I was sitting in a restaurant with Kristen, a good friend of mine who is also a child of divorce. We were having lunch together and our conversation shifted to my experiences living with Ivy and Eve. Kristen began to relate similar problems she had had in the past with her stepfather, Bill, and stepbrother, Daniel. It was interesting to me, as many of the difficulties and situations we had encountered were so similar. We really bonded. Halfway through our conversation, I remember sharing a laugh together as we both came to the same realization about how to deal with things when new family members enter your life. It is important to start with a friendship before you can build a relationship.

Brother to Brother

I love my brother, Wes. As we were growing up, we had a typical brother relationship. We played, we fought, we teased each other—but when things were difficult for one of us, the other was there. When our parents separated and Wes moved in with Mom, it utterly changed our relationship.

Ever since the day Wes left with Mom, guilt has lingered inside me. I worry that I put him in a position where he felt obligated to go with her because I was staying with Dad. I thought I was protecting him in my attempt to fight for the family, but I never talked with him about why I chose to stay with Dad. I often wondered if he resented me for it, as my decision initiated the beginning of the gap that was created in our relationship—a gap that I didn't know how to fix or talk to him about. Our communication about important things became almost non-existent, as we continually chose to keep our emotions under lock and key. I felt like a part of me went missing when I lost Wes, because we too became divided. We weren't involved in each other's lives anymore, and in a weird way it felt like we were on different teams.

The divorce presented the same situation for both of us and we faced many of the same challenges. And yet we reacted very differently. Although I can't speak for Wes, I believe we felt many of the same things. However, we each had our own path to walk and journey to endure. Interestingly, I lived with Dad and many of my issues came from my anger towards Mom, whereas Wes lived with Mom and seemed to have more issues with Dad.

I missed terribly how our relationship used to be. Every day was different when Wes wasn't around. Everything we used to do together completely stopped. When I woke up in the morning, I didn't fight with Wes about the hot water in the shower. We didn't scrap at the breakfast table. Our days of coming home from school, making a bowl of ice cream, and watching the Flintstones and the Jetsons together were over. When I did see Wes, the spirit and the brotherly love we had shared were gone too. We didn't fight or tease each other, and the days of me calling him "Westil Leibellnachuck" were long gone. Our relationship took on a serious tone. I resented the fact that we didn't have the same amount of time to do things together, and I often felt confused about whether I should be mad at Mom and Dad for that or mad at myself. When Wes and me talked, it was usually to ask, "How are you doing? What's new?" The other would answer, "Good. Nothing much." I learned more about Wes through talking with his friends and Mom and Dad. Everything changed, and a whole new relationship needed to form in order for us to bond and get to know each other again.

For a long time, I wanted to talk to Wes and find out his thoughts, but in the beginning I just couldn't. I was trying to set an example of being strong, and at the time I believed that meant sucking it up and taking it like a man. It was hard for me to share my feelings with him and tell him that I was hurting. I didn't want Wes to see weakness in me. I just wanted him to be proud of me, and I didn't want to let him down. Inside, I know it would have helped me to hug him and tell him how much I missed him and how much I didn't want the divorce to tear us apart. However, when I got the chance, I backed out. It took me a long time to recognize what was really important to me, and I realized that my pride was getting in the way of Wes and me having a relationship.

I had become confused about my role as the older brother, and I no longer knew my place. I didn't know what Wes really needed from me and I wasn't sure what I needed from him. However, because I always thought I had to act strong in Wes' presence, I felt I needed to be more of a parent than a brother to him, and make sure he was doing the right things. I'm sure he resented me for some of the lectures I tried to unload on him, and I soon realized that wasn't what he wanted or needed. We both wanted a brother and a friend.

When I did eventually go and live at Mom's, it felt like Wes and me had to start all over again. We both had our own lives by then, and it no longer felt like we were involved in each other's world. In order to rebuild the closeness we once had, we needed to form a new relationship and reconnect by becoming friends all over again. It was extremely difficult, as so many things had built up and we had both changed. I feel that over the years, Wes and me have found our own ways to connect, although sometimes it takes great effort on both of our parts to do so.

For me, this has been difficult to write about because many unresolved issues continue to linger. There are feelings and issues that Wes and me have yet to discuss, and I still find it difficult to talk to him about them. A valuable lesson I have learned, one that has helped me open up to Wes and start to build the relationship I have always wanted to have with him, is to acknowledge that we need to make the effort to bridge the gap that has come between us. We need to realize why that is so important.

I know that with time, Wes and me will continue to develop a stronger relationship and bring back the fun and involvement we used to share.

CHAPTER EIGHT

Resolving Issues

"Loss is sometimes necessary in order to learn the truth."
~Wesley Mark Leibel

Mom asked, "Craig, is it more important to be right or to love?" Her words deflated my angry rage as I slowly let my body sink into her couch. She had been listening to how upset I was with Trina over an issue we were in a deadlock with; we had been fighting about it for several months. It was creating a tremendous strain on our marriage. We butted heads, too stubborn to give in as we tried to prove one of us was right and the other was wrong. The issue had been blown way out of proportion, and our fight had evolved from a minor dispute to lashing out with fierce direct insults back and forth. Now, it had become an obsession for me to make Trina see the light and realize she was wrong. The reason for our feud was irrelevant to our personal relationship, as it was about a situation that involved other people in the family. It only affected us indirectly, so it shouldn't have had any real bearing on Trina and me. Yet it was tearing us apart and weighing heavily on our future together, as issues from past disputes entered into the picture, compounding our anger and stubbornness.

That night, I said, "I just don't understand it, Mom. I can't see how Trina doesn't get it. It's so obvious. She knows I'm right and yet she doesn't do anything but continue to start a fight." That statement irked Mom. She tilted her head back and took a deep breath; then she went for the jugular by unloading the question on me: "Is it more important to be right or to love?" I had never asked myself that question before, and it really hit home. I had been spending so much time trying to be right, and trying to change Trina, that I forgot what was really important. Mom continued, "Craig, it took me a long time to learn that in a relationship, each partner needs to be responsible for his or her feelings, anger, or issues. It is important to remember to own your part of the conflict first, without placing blame. You have to know what you are responsible for in order to find a resolution. Perhaps if your Dad and I had known that, things would have turned out differently."

As I listened to my mom talk, I connected with her message. It tugged at my heart, and I started to look differently at what Trina and I were fighting about. The tension, anxiety, and anger I had been feeling began to melt away and turn into regret as I remembered how much I still loved my wife. All of a sudden, I could see the truth shining through the mess of confusion I had created. When I let go of the idea of having to be right and simply tried to understand what Trina needed from me, it didn't matter who was right. All that mattered was that we could still care about each other even though we disagreed. We could still love each other for who we were.

Driving home from Mom's, I really started to question why I was so mad with Trina and how come it became so important to me to prove I was right. What did I want to achieve with that? I didn't know if it just involved my ego or if it was something else. I knew it had started out being about my ego, but deep down I could feel it had evolved into much more. It was about going against some of my beliefs and facing some of my unresolved issues about relationships. Underneath, it was also about my underlying need to know the reasons why Trina loved me. I still had an immense fear that one day she would leave me, just as Mom had left Dad. I felt that I couldn't give in to her regarding our disagreement because if I did, it would leave me vulnerable. I didn't want to be vulnerable because I felt that would somehow make me less of a person and unworthy of her love.

I knew in that moment that I was wrong. I realized my fear was so strong that I was actually driving Trina to leave me, but I didn't understand my behavior. It was almost like I was testing her and trying to find a guarantee, rather than just loving her. I didn't know how to fix what I had just destroyed with all of our fighting, but I knew if I wanted my marriage to work, it was time to resolve some of my issues so we could start to go on with our lives again.

As I pulled into the driveway of our home, I wasn't sure how to start the conversation or how to go about setting ground rules to prevent our discussion from sparking a fight. Should I walk in and confront Trina head-on? Walk in and say I was sorry? I felt so stupid about all the demands I had put on her to tell me her feelings, and about the explanations I had given her for why we should talk about things—how important it was to be open and truthful and listen to one another. And here I was, stuck trying to take my own advice and come to terms with myself. Sometimes in life, our greatest strengths can also be our greatest weaknesses when we have to bear the responsibility for them.

Scared to admit I had been wrong, I slowly walked into the house and went into the bedroom. Trina had been waiting up, wondering where I had gone after I stormed off. We sat quietly together, each waiting for the other to open the conversation, when I saw in her eyes what I had been searching for all along—love. I extended my hand to hers as I whispered, "I'm sorry, Trina … I love you," and gave her a hug. She looked up at me and said, "I love you, too. Where have you been?" I paused for a moment and as a smile of regret grew on my face, I asked, "Trina, is it more important to be right or to love?"

The Lingering Pain

Divorce can bring pain and scars, and it also can create a lingering pain. The first time I realized my lingering pain was years after my parents' divorce, when I tried to support my friend, Hannah, after her parents broke up. As she spoke, I became enraged and discovered that I was still harboring deep resentment and bitterness about my parents' divorce. It had been affecting my attitude and behavior and I had let it take control of many decisions I was making in my life. The lingering pain came upon me by surprise, and I never realized how hard it would be to let go of. I still carry some of it with me every day.

～

It was about 9:00 PM on a Sunday night. The phone rang and it was Hannah. She was crying hysterically and sounded furious. I could hardly understand what she was saying through her mumbled ranting. I asked her to calm down, take a deep breath, and tell me what had happened. She paused and the phone went silent for a moment. Then I heard the words slowly tumble from her mouth, "Craig ... my dad had an affair ... and my parents are getting a divorce."

Surprised and stunned by the news, I couldn't come up with a response. I could feel my body tense and butterflies formed in the pit of my stomach. I became incredibly nervous and stuck for words. I couldn't believe this was happening to Hannah. So many emotions attacked me all at once! I felt transported back in time to the day that my parents unleashed the news about their separation. Just as it had back then, only one question echoed in my mind: Why? I realized in that moment how the people I was close to must have felt when my parents split up. I felt so helpless as I tried to think of the right thing to say to calm Hannah and make her feel better. She was still crying, and all I could come up with was, "Everything will be okay, Hannah. You will be okay."

She asked if I would come and pick her up because she didn't want to spend another minute in the house with her dad. I grabbed my coat and my keys and headed out the door. On the way over there, I felt dumbfounded and angrier than I could ever remember feeling. I thought to myself, *Why? Why does this have to happen?!* I don't know who I was angrier with—Hannah's dad for doing what he did, the world for allowing divorce, or my parents for splitting up.

Hannah was alone, sobbing as she waited for me on the front step of her house. I pulled up into the driveway and got out of the car. She ran over and put her arms around me as she stammered out questions: "Craig, what should I do? What's going to happen? My mom is so mad; I'm scared she might do something. I don't know where she went. I just hate my dad for doing this. How could he?" She squeezed me tight and I could feel the anger start to steam inside me as we got into the car. I knew she needed me just to listen and let her know I cared about her, but I couldn't help feeling enraged.

We drove around town as I let Hannah cry until she felt like talking. I could see the pain and devastation in her eyes. Like me, she'd had no idea or suspicion that her parents had problems, and she was in complete shock. After her tears dried, she said, "I'm so scared. I don't know what to do. What can I do to fix this, Craig? What did you do when your parents told you?" Hannah's question brought to mind the vivid memory of sitting at the kitchen table as the words rolled off Mom's lips: "We're splitting up." As much as I wanted to be there for Hannah, I felt consumed by emotions. It took everything I had not to explode. I couldn't believe Hannah was sitting across from me, at the threshold of a journey that I had fought so hard with. I wanted to shield her, fix it, take her away, and help her avoid all that was about to come. I wished I had a magic wand to wave and make everything better for her, but I knew it wasn't that simple.

Hannah was heartbroken and I wanted to say all the right things. I started to rant, bombarding her with my issues and how I had to deal with my hurt. I was trying to tell her it would be okay, but all kinds of other bitter comments were coming out of my mouth. I said, "Hannah, you can't control any of this or fix it. There's nothing you can do; it's not your problem or your fault. You will have to be strong in order to survive." After I calmed down and scared the heck out of her, I looked over and could see in her eyes that she was begging to know things were going to be okay. I felt so guilty for forgetting why I was there and for instead trying to solve all of her problems. I said, "I'm sorry, Hannah, I don't know what came over me." Even though she said it was good to listen to me, I knew I wasn't much help.

As Hannah turned to stare through the window, I could feel my eyes start to water. She was such a nice girl, full of energy and life. She was the kind of person everyone liked and wanted to be around. We would laugh, joke, and have good times together. But now she sat in front of me, looking shattered, her whole spirit crushed. It was heart wrenching for me to see her so upset, and I knew inside that it had only just begun. I realized I wasn't the best person to be supporting her that night, as my emotions got the best of me. I gave her a hug and apologized again, promising I would just listen.

She didn't know exactly how or why it happened, but when she got home from school that day, her parents were screaming and yelling at each other. Through the fighting, Hannah found out her dad had been unfaithful. Her mom demanded a divorce, then left the house, telling her husband he had better be gone when she got back. Hannah's parents were great people and they had such a nice family. It felt so tragic to me. I listened to her talk about how shocked and mad she felt, and how she hated her dad for betraying her mom and her. At the same time, she was confused and felt guilty because she still didn't want her dad to leave.

On my way home, I felt completely mixed up. I was filled with a lingering sense of pain and a hollow aching feeling, knowing there were things I needed to deal with that I was too scared to face. When I arrived home, I talked with my mom about what had happened with Hannah and about how I felt lost in my emotions. I told her how mad I got and how I had bombarded Hannah with my own anger instead of being more supportive. To comfort me, Mom said, "Well, Craig, sometimes in life we teach what we most need to learn. Maybe you needed Hannah, too."

Through the years, I have found what Mom said to be true. I have been fortunate to talk with many friends who, like me, have been through their parents' divorce. Each time, I discovered more insights and these have helped me tackle and overcome my fears. There is comfort in knowing that we are all struggling through it together.

Why Open Old Wounds?

Why would you want to bring back an old wound or relive a painful memory? The answer is to allow yourself to heal. We all choose the events in our lives that we want to store as memories, good and bad, and we all decide what we are willing to deal with, let go of, or hang onto. If we choose to bury our painful memories in an attempt to protect ourselves from our fear and hurt, we may find that this will haunt us and control our actions throughout our lives.

As time progressed and the years passed by, I buried many painful memories and scars. I didn't want to have to deal with them, because for the most part, I was simply fed up with all of it. I didn't realize that those issues would turn into lingering pain. Have you ever been really angry with someone for something that happened a long time ago, but instead of dealing with it, you tucked it away somewhere in the back of your mind? Then in an innocent conversation, a neutral party might say something to spark your anger. Suddenly your body starts to shake and vibrate, your heart races as though you're ready to explode in anger, and the most foolish thing you have ever said comes out of your mouth. You then walk around for the next several days, kicking yourself as you play the situation over in your head like a broken record. I have been there many times.

For me, dealing with unresolved issues became important because I didn't want to continue to live in misery or fear. I wanted to have all of the things in my life that I longed for. I discovered that the only way I could do this would be to heal my wounds so that they couldn't prevent me from taking action with my life. One of the biggest lessons the divorce taught me was to face my fears clearly and directly. I needed to attack them head-on by affirming their source so that I could take back the control in my life.

I believe that there are two kinds of unresolved issues. First, there are issues that I have with others. I know I will have to confront these sooner or later in order to conquer them and bring peace and resolution to my life before they eat me up. Second, there are issues that I believe I need to resolve privately within myself, because it wouldn't make a positive difference in my life if I were to confront them with others. For instance, certain family members that I love have different beliefs or issues with my parents' divorce. This can enrage me; however, a confrontation would only create worse problems, and it's not worth losing the relationship over. I needed to make peace with these issues in my own way in order to let go of them. Regardless of how we choose to resolve our issues and heal our lingering pain, it's important to remember to first determine the outcome we want to achieve.

Carrying unresolved issues around can be very destructive to our lives. We give up control when we allow ourselves to be dominated by hurtful feelings. They will influence our decisions in life, in both good and bad ways. Many times I found myself biting my tongue when someone said something that would irritate me, and I chose to bottle up my emotions. The more I did so, the more miserable I became. This resulted in me unintentionally redirecting my pain at others, something I didn't want to do.

Over the years, after many unproductive angry rants, I have learned the hard way that there are two key elements to resolving issues. First, ask to be heard when you talk and respect others by really listening to how they feel. Ask them to clarify what they say if need be. Secondly, it's equally important to listen to ourselves to find the truth about how we feel. What works best for me is to explain my feelings honestly and directly with the people I have issues with. We can then work towards a common goal we would all like to achieve.

Through my experience, as hard as it has been, I realized I had to allow myself to become vulnerable to my fears and pain in order to let them go. The only way I knew how to do this was to bring it all back—to relive it, but change it. At first, I found myself reliving the same pain over and over again, because I didn't know to ask myself two questions: What can I learn from this? What can I do to change it in order to let it go? Through taking a new perspective, changing my attitude, and looking to forgive, I was able to own my mistakes, take responsibility for my feelings, and find the lessons I needed to resolve some of the hurt.

Being Vulnerable

I remember the first time I decided I had to break up with Trina, back when we were dating. It was then that I began to realize I was going to have to risk leaving myself vulnerable in order to be loved. This was despite the protective shell I had wrapped around myself over the years—which Trina was slowly breaking away by challenging me to face the shadows that lingered in my life.

Trina had had other boyfriends before we met, just as I had been with other girlfriends. However, I had a much harder time accepting that fact than she did. I was insecure with relationships as it was, and when I started to fall in love with Trina, it all of a sudden became very important to me to know that it was me she wanted to be with. I wanted concrete reasoning to guarantee she would never leave.

The problem came between Trina and me because of the way I handled my fear, especially with my inability to trust. I had stored up many unresolved issues relating to relationships, and had never dealt with allowing myself to trust someone. These were issues I didn't even know I had until I fell into a situation and they made themselves present. Then they were like firecrackers inside me, coming from every direction all at once. I unloaded it all on Trina with my intense mood swings. I found that my insecurity about her ex-boyfriends triggered my emotions and I started getting mad at her for things she did long before she met me. I started comparing myself to the others and feeling jealous of her past; I was unable to trust why she was with me.

The closer we became, the worse I got. My fear grew and I couldn't handle what was going on inside me. I was driving Trina away, picking at her with question upon question. I kept trying to find some kind of inaccuracy to pin on her, until she became fearful of telling me anything. Our relationship grew intolerable and we were both walking on eggshells, waiting for the one comment that might cause me to erupt. One minute I could be the man of her dreams, and the next minute I was someone she couldn't stand.

I knew it was wrong. I knew I was losing someone I wanted to be with because of my fear, but it was so strong and had so much control over me at the time that it didn't matter. It was almost like I wanted to prove I was right, that Trina would just leave me in the end. It was the stupidest thing, and yet I was doing it because of the pain and betrayal I had felt when Mom left. As much as I never wanted to hurt Trina, I ended up doing so anyway. The truth was that I didn't believe I could trust women.

The day finally came when Trina lied to me. Her stories were getting all twisted and filled with holes after my endless questioning. I never gave her a real chance to talk to me. By this time in our relationship, she was scared to tell me anything.

It was raining outside and we were in the kitchen of a townhouse I was renting. We were talking and joking around when I started casually probing to find the missing pieces to some of her stories. I asked a question about a particular guy who had mysteriously shown up at Trina's house one afternoon a few weeks earlier. It had surprised him when I answered her door. After he left, Trina quickly told me that he was only a friend who wanted to say hello, and that I should ignore it. Of course, that wasn't good enough for me and I knew there had to be more to that story.

I was right. I found out that morning that he was a previous boyfriend. I caught Trina off-guard as I jumped all over her in a vicious rage. She quickly tried to defend herself by stating, "I told you that already." But it was too late for any talk. She had lied, I had caught her, and my mind was made up. It was over and I wanted her out of the house and out of my life. A huge fight erupted between us as I told her to leave and accused her of being a liar. Trina protested and explained that it was an innocent, unexpected visit, and that she had been scared to tell me about their past. I looked her in the eye and asked, "What would have happened if I hadn't been there that day?" She said, "Nothing. I'm sorry I didn't tell you." Upset, I didn't buy it. I opened the door and shouted at her, "I want you to leave right now!"

She left in tears and it was over. I sat and watched the rain through the window, asking myself, "Did I do the right thing or did I just lose someone I truly love?" I kept questioning things back and forth in my mind. If she lied to me about that, what else might she be lying about ... loving me? How could I ever trust her again? When I asked myself that question, I began to wonder if I ever had trusted Trina.

The truth was that I didn't want her to leave and I didn't want to break up. I wanted to put an end to the nightmare I was living inside. I wanted to know I could trust Trina. I wanted to know she loved me as I loved her. I didn't want to keep putting demands on her, but it was the only way I felt she could prove her love. I began to feel heartbroken as I realized I was the problem in our relationship. Because of how clouded I had been with my own emotions, I had lost the woman I loved.

I wanted to call and make things right, but I didn't, and she didn't call me either. I spent the next few days confused and full of sorrow, wishing I could talk to her. Finally, I got fed up with pacing by the phone, waiting for it to ring. I decided to call her. Just as I was dialing the numbers, the doorbell rang and it was Trina. She asked to come in and said she had something to say. She let me have it! I could barely take a breath between her sentences. She laid it all on the line, telling me she loved me, wanted to be with me, and was sorry if she had hurt me—but that she was not going to take anymore of my junk. It had to stop! If I couldn't love her for who she was, then she didn't want to be with me. Before I had a chance to say anything in response, she left, telling me to think about what I really wanted and to let her know. Wow, I got what was coming to me and she was right about all of it.

I was overwhelmed and scared. I had a chance to make things right, but I didn't know how. I wanted to tell her so many things, but I didn't want us to fight. I just wanted to tell her how I really felt— that I loved her and was sorry—and explain what was happening to me. I decided to write her a letter and put it all on the line, just as she had done. I needed to be vulnerable and open up, despite my fears about how she would respond. After Trina read the letter and we talked about what each of us had said, we grew closer and stronger as a couple. It wasn't easy and we still had a long road to go before we could mend all the hurt and wounds we had created.

I knew that moving on in our relationship would be a big task for us. I had to bring back some painful memories and risk being vulnerable in order for us to love and trust each other. I really didn't know if I could. But if I didn't, I knew I would never get what I wanted. I would have to let Trina go, and to me that would be much more tragic.

Do I Believe in Divorce?

This is a hard question for a child of divorce to answer. Every situation is individual and unique, and I'm certainly not one to judge other people's situations without knowing the facts. I believe sometimes divorce is necessary, but it is naturally never an easy thing to go through. I also believe that not all marriages that end in divorce have to end that way. I believe divorce to be the last option for a married couple, and I believe in the importance of family.

No one should ever have to live in an unhealthy relationship or a bad situation. Children and families shouldn't be forced to live with painful circumstances such as physical or verbal abuse, addiction problems, or lies and deception. I believe there needs to be an alternative for a better life, and sometimes divorce can provide the answer.

However, at the same time, I feel that many people have made divorce an easy solution to their difficulties, and sometimes it might not be necessary. For some people in today's world, it has almost become the thing to do. If it feels good, do it, and if it feels bad, get out of it. I don't agree with people who choose to divorce simply because of their selfish needs, without regard for the consequences or the impact it will have on their children. Divorce is a drastic decision for anyone to have to make, and there are huge circumstances to weigh. I believe the decision to divorce should be made if it will benefit everyone in the family in the long-term. But before it is made, I think a couple should place real value on their lives and family and consider that there are many alternative options to dealing with problems in a relationship.

&

In my case, I see my family as one that won through the divorce journey because even when divided, we never stopped being a family. Although it came with horrendous consequences and I will always wish my parents had never divorced, I believe Mom and Dad are both better off for it today. However, this is only because they have both owned up to the mistakes they made, taken time to work on their issues, and profited from their lessons by putting them into practice. They took responsibility for the parts they played in the divorce and by doing that, they have become stronger and better people.

Mom once concluded to me that the biggest reason they are divorced today is that at the time they separated, they didn't have the necessary skills to correct their destructive patterns and make things work. It was too big, too painful, and required efforts beyond their capabilities at that time. Their relationship was more about being right than loving each other, and because of that they never found any resolution to their problems or agreement on solutions. They never faced the truth or took responsibility for the part each of them was playing in their relationship. They just didn't know how to resolve their issues, and it got to the point where they never would be able to do so.

In many ways, I know I am a better person today because of the divorce. It certainly taught me important lessons about love, marriage, and relationships. Ironically, I learned more from the mistakes my parents made and my own trial-and-error process. However, as excruciating as it was to learn these lessons, they have made me a stronger person. The divorce challenged me to examine who I really was, and I discovered I could love myself for the things that were real about me.

I have grown considerably and learned many other invaluable life lessons. I have grown closer to my parents and Wes, and I have a deeper appreciation for love and my life. Would I say I am better off that my parents divorced? For the most part, no. It sounds contradictory after describing the many lessons I have learned and the feeling I have of being a better person. However, at times such as Christmas, my children's birthdays, weddings, and important family functions, I am reminded of the family I know in my heart I would still always rather have.

The most important thing I believe is that no matter what the situation, it is vital that we acknowledge our loss, recognize our need for healing, and choose to spend time resolving difficult issues in order to move on with our lives.

CHAPTER NINE
Letting Go

"No one but you can take away your heart and soul."
~Darin Kowalchuk

I will never forget the day I asked Trina to marry me. We had been dating for almost three years, and one day it hit me like a ton of bricks—the defining moment. I could not imagine my life without her in it. I had to be connected to her and I needed to love her. I felt it, I knew it, and I wanted it! I wanted to spend the rest of my life with her. However, somewhere inside, intense deep-rooted emotions were popping issues into my head like popcorn kernels. My insides were screaming, *Don't do it! Are you completely nuts? You know exactly what's going to happen!* These thoughts had been plaguing me, dragging me down to defeat about the mere idea of marriage. I couldn't let go of the pain and the fear.

Trina and I were both from small towns, which were unfortunately on opposite ends of the big city. That meant about an hour's drive between our homes. Driving back and forth, sometimes twice a day, was getting to be too overwhelming for us—even with Trina's parents' kind gesture of allowing me to stay over many nights in their guest room. (I think, though, that their motives were probably more to keep me in check, rather than just to make a nice gesture!)

After years of the back-and-forth chaos, the time came when

our dating relationship was beginning to develop into something more serious. Trina and I felt it would be in our best interests to move in together—get a place of our own, eliminate the driving, and take the next step in our relationship. Instead of really thinking about what we were doing, we lost ourselves in the romance. We jumped in feet-first and took the plunge, moving into a small basement suite in the city. It was small, but as Trina put it, "cozy."

It was a cold winter day in the basement suite—December 21, 1994 to be exact. It appeared to begin as a typical routine day, just like any other. Trina and I got up in the morning, had breakfast, and parted to go off to work. However, it was anything but typical. The previous night, we had had a big fight! It was about everything we could think of, a huge blow-up. We were both stressed about work, money, living arrangements, and our relationship, and this turned into a royal battle of us taking our frustrations out on each other. All the little things had built up to a boil, annoying habits were making themselves present, and both of us were seriously on edge, learning about the "fun" in living together.

At breakfast we didn't speak, but Trina's eyes told me she had passed her tolerance level and was doing some deep thinking. Truthfully, the fight was about more than just the little digs we had thrown at each other all night. Something was missing for us and we could both feel it. I didn't want to admit it to myself, but I knew it was about the big M word: Marriage!

We had talked about getting married many times before, but I never took it too seriously. I always turned it into some kind of joke or changed the subject, because I didn't even want to think about how scared I was to actually get married! It terrified me and I didn't believe I was even capable of making a marriage work, especially after all the garbage my parents went through with their divorce. There was no way I wanted that or wanted my kids to go through it.

I had developed an attitude towards marriage: "Who needs it?!" I was petrified that my wife would just end up leaving me in the end. For years I was convinced I would never get married, but Trina would often hint at it. It was driving me absolutely crazy. She was determined to make me see the light.

As I sat at the breakfast table, looking into Trina's eyes, I was reminded of what my mom had told me a few years after they divorced. She said, "When a relationship gets really rough and you find you're fighting about all kinds of things that don't make much sense, it is usually a call to action—a call to move closer, grow together, and fall more deeply in love."

It was becoming obvious to me that Trina and I needed to come together, work out some issues, and make the next step—the marriage commitment—or move on. I felt like I was in a pressure cooker! Usually this was my cue to say, "It's been great, but I think we just want different things in life. Let's stay friends," and move on, because I would never be ready. And yet as hard as I tried, I couldn't bring myself to say it.

The truth was that I had been trying to break up with Trina for months, but I just couldn't do it. I didn't want to. Even though my brain was telling me it was time to end it, my heart had emotions exploding inside of me like firecrackers! I was a complete mess! I couldn't say anything to Trina about it because I was embarrassed, thinking she wouldn't understand my fear. I worried that she would just laugh at me or say something like, "What kind of man are you?"

A Flash of Insight

After I left for work that morning, I had this overwhelming feeling: It's now or never. I knew this was it. I had to make a decision before I destroyed our relationship. It wasn't fair to Trina. I began to ask myself, "What's going on with you, Craig? You're a mess. What's the truth here?" I needed to make sense of my confusion. I needed to pinpoint what exactly I was so scared of and what was stopping me from asking Trina to marry me. Something was making me so mad and so crazy, and I knew deep down it wasn't all the little things we had been fighting about. It was something else. I got an indescribable, pestering feeling in my stomach from time to time, especially when I started to feel like I wanted to get closer to Trina. That feeling would not let me forget my belief that marriage was a bad thing. It had me. It would protect me by shooting messages to my brain, such as, "Marriage is not for you!" It had been lingering inside me for a long, long time and I had let it have complete control of my actions.

That's when it hit me! I knew what was really bothering me! It was the control my parents' divorce had over me and the hatred I had towards myself for allowing it to control my life. In that moment, everything I had been bottling up started to unravel. I had been avoiding the fact that I really didn't feel right about living with Trina out of wedlock. What I really wanted was to build a life with her and ask her to marry me. But instead of moving towards what I wanted, I had been resisting, rationalizing how I felt and dismissing my true feelings in order to avoid the pain of being scared. I spent all my time finding fault in the relationship, Trina, and myself, and I was missing out on enjoying the love I actually had.

A sudden flash pierced my thoughts: *Ask her to marry you!* What? Wow, I went numb. My body started shaking. The feeling was so strong that I couldn't avoid it. I wanted to get married. After years of telling myself that it was a stupid idea, I actually wanted to do it! It was overpowering my every thought. My mind and emotions were moving so fast. I started to feel alive for the first time in so long. Unable to drive, I had to pull off the road and park in order to collect my thoughts. I shouted, smiling to myself, "Marriage? No way! Not me!" Then, the ultimate question entered my mind: "How should I ask?"

As I attempted to figure out the best way, I began to have an argument with myself. It was like I had a little devil and a little angel sitting on my shoulders:

"Craig, don't be an idiot! Do you really want to end up like your parents?"

"Craig, you know you love her and she loves you. Why not have some happiness in your life?"

"Happiness? Ha! You know better than to believe that line. You don't deserve to be happy!"

"Why not? Why don't you deserve to be happy? What have you ever done? It wasn't your fault your parents divorced. You're not your parents. You're you, and you have your own life!"

Then the thought crossed my mind, for the first time in my life: *What if I could make a marriage work? What if I could have the things I want, and have a loving family?* I held onto that thought as the little devil mysteriously went *Puff!* and disappeared. And the little angel smiled.

Shivers shot down my spine and my body started to quiver. I began to feel immensely excited and nervous. Then, amazingly, I noticed I was parked in front of a limousine company. Inside the building sat the most incredible limousine I had ever seen. My plan to ask Trina to marry me started to hatch before my eyes! Mom was right: God will provide. Trina and I both loved limousines and this one was like something out of a fairytale! She would love it! My plan was coming together all at once. My heart was racing faster than it ever had before! I knew what I really wanted and how I was going to get it. I also knew at that moment that it was time for me to let go of the pain, risk my heart, and let trust and love into my life.

I felt invincible! I decided I wasn't going to let my past control me anymore. I wasn't going to let my fears and doubts about marriage consume me. I would let go of the pain. I would no longer push away the people I loved. I was going to make my mark! My parents' divorce was not going to control my life decisions any longer. I was taking back my life and deciding my own future. I wanted to live my own life, make my own mistakes, achieve my own successes, and just live! I was going to let go and trust my instincts and the love I felt. I knew Trina was everything I always wanted. All I needed to do was trust in myself, in her, and in us—and ask!

It took me years to build up the walls I had protecting me. It was a safe place, a place where I wouldn't get hurt or even worse, hurt someone else. But it was also a lonely, unsatisfying place where fear controlled me. As vulnerable as I felt about risking my heart, I had way more to gain than to lose. Imagine … a life of living in love and not in fear!

I picked up my cell phone to call work and let them know I wouldn't be in. Then, nervously, I got out of my truck and opened the door to the limousine rental company. It was time to put my plan into action.

I only had about seven hours to get the plan into place. The first step was to rent the limousine of my dreams. As I waited to talk with the manager, I went and sat on the car's plush leather seats. The limousine held up to eleven passengers. It had a television, full bar, phone, complete stereo system, leather seats in the back, a plush couch along the side, and a sunroof. It was designed with sheer elegance and was the longest limousine I had ever seen. It was in mint condition and to top it off, it had the decorative trimmings of a Rolls Royce. I began to daydream about the expression Trina would have on her face as I got down on one knee and proposed. What would she say? I visualized us riding in style, celebrating our engagement.

Imagining her smile reminded me of the day we first met, back in college. I had the exclusive opportunity of holding the parkade elevator door open as Trina rushed in, getting out of the cold winter air. She was flustered and had rosy cheeks as she gave me a positively beautiful smile and whispered, "Thank you." We rode the elevator to the top floor, exchanging glances without saying a word. I could see a small smile tucked away on the side of her face as she tried to not look directly at me. The elevator stopped abruptly and I motioned for her to go first.

We both walked away in different directions. Halfway to my truck, I just had to look back to see if she was looking. (The dating test! If she was looking, I knew she was interested.) Casually, I glanced over my shoulder, trying not to look obvious. I caught a glimpse of her smile as she swung around to make it appear that she wasn't looking. I smiled to myself, knowing I had her interest! Although nothing was said, that was our first moment together. I couldn't wait to see that beautiful smile again.

The general manager came over to the limousine with some bad news. He said it had already been rented for the night. I couldn't believe it. I had walked in feeling like I was on top of the world and *bang*—I suddenly fell off. It took me way too long to reach this point emotionally, and there was no way I was turning back now. I had to have the limo and I wasn't going to give up! I explained my plan, pleading my case to the manager, but he wouldn't budge. I asked to see the owner. I waited for about fifteen minutes, strategizing the rest of my plan and staring at the limousine. Every hair on my body was standing on end with excitement. The owner finally came down to express his apologies, because the car had been rented to their best customer for the whole afternoon and night. Ah…! I lowered my head and began protesting, deciding to go for the heartstrings. I told him I was going to propose to my girlfriend and that we were a young couple, just starting out. I said that this limousine would be symbolic to fulfilling our dreams together, and that it would be so fitting to carry Trina off in style. She would love it!

I said, "There must be something we can do. I only need it for an hour, maybe two." The owner asked, "Does it really have to be today?" I said, "Yes! It has to be today!" I felt it in my heart, my soul, all the way down to my toes! He felt my enthusiasm and said he could try to work it out with his client. He suggested that perhaps the client could take in dinner during the time I needed the limousine.

"Great!" I shouted, wondering in the back of mind how much this would cost me, now that he had me right where he wanted me. All I can say is we negotiated a steep but fair price, on the grounds that the client would agree. I took out my Visa card and paid the owner in good faith that he would find a way to make it work.

While I was waiting impatiently for the limousine owner to call me, I had a million things to do. I needed to purchase a ring and champagne. I needed to call my parents, Trina's parents, my brother, and her sisters. My idea was to meet Trina back at our place, propose, and then take the limousine out in style. We would pick up our family members to announce the big news and celebrate.

My first stop was the jeweler's to buy the ring Trina had hinted to me about a few months prior. I knew it was the one she really wanted. However, when I arrived at the jewelry store, I couldn't believe it! They were closed. The store was in a mall in the city, and it was the middle of the day. How in the heck could they be closed? I wasn't sure what to do. This was the ring Trina had to have. I waited for about twenty minutes, contemplating what I should do. I had asked around, and none of the other merchants knew why the jewelry store was closed.

Finally, I decided to go to another store and try to find a similar ring. I ran back to my truck in the parking lot and as I was fishing through my pocket for my keys, I realized I must have forgotten my cell phone on the bench in front of the jewelry store. Upset, I quickly ran back and to my surprise, the owner had just arrived to unlock the front door of the store. I was amazed! Had I not forgotten my cell phone, I would have been long gone. I walked into the store and bought the ring. Just feeling the box in my pocket sent butterflies swirling through my stomach.

I started making my phone calls to invite the family members, disguising my plan by suggesting I would be picking them up for a special Christmas dinner surprise. First, I called Trina's parents. Of course, they already had plans and it took some fast-talking persuasion to make sure they would be there without revealing my surprise. I knew that would be important to Trina. Next I called her sisters, who were ecstatic about the dinner surprise and added the extra push to help cancel their parents' plans. They were all to meet at my soon-to-be sister-in-law's house, where we would pick them up and surprise them with the limousine and our big news. They had no idea what they were in store for.

Next to invite was my dad. I visited him at his work and invited him to the Christmas dinner. He too had plans. I could not seem to catch a break. It was his girlfriend's birthday and he was taking her out for supper. I told him, "Dad, I just can't seem to win today." So I had to let him in on the secret to ensure he would be there. We decided I would pick both him and his girlfriend up at the restaurant after they finished eating.

That left my mom and brother. When I called Wes, he wasn't home. I figured he was probably still at work, so I decided to drive to Mom's house and meet up with him there because he was sure to be home soon. I knew it would be harder for him to say no in person. On my way, I stopped off and bought champagne and roses. When I arrived at my mom's, Wes was preparing to go to a party with a date he did not want to break. Again, I had to promise that it would be a surprise he would never forget, which convinced him. Due to the shortage of time, Wes agreed to arrange to bring Mom.

I was on my way home to set up the scene when my cell phone rang. It was the limousine owner. He said he put in a message with his driver, because he couldn't reach his client by phone. He was waiting to hear back, but he was confident that the driver would take care of it. I gave him our address and hoped for the best!

I put the phone down and suddenly remembered I was supposed to meet my grandma for a Christmas appetizer after work that day. I figured I still had enough time to make it to the restaurant, have a quick visit, and beat Trina home to set up. I had made plans with my grandma weeks ago and I couldn't break them. She was already waiting at a booth when I walked into the restaurant. I apologized for being late, revealing parts of my plan to her as I sat down. We talked for a few minutes and she congratulated me, passing on some words of wisdom before sending me home to quickly get ready.

Will You Marry Me?

The time finally came and my plan was set. I just needed to get home and prepare for the big moment. I wasn't sure if everything would come together, but I had faith on my side and was bound and determined. As I drove up to our place, I couldn't believe it: Trina had come home early, today of all days! I thought to myself, *Unbelievable. What a day I'm having!* Now I would have to improvise a little to get the champagne, ring, and roses inside. It was a good thing I was wearing my overcoat so that I could hide them as I walked in.

Trina was watching television as I walked past, trying to look inconspicuous. I hurried over to the fridge to sneak the champagne in, then put the roses in the cupboard. Trina startled me by yelling from the couch, "Craig, what are you doing?" I quickly grabbed a Coke out of the fridge and said, "Oh, just getting a drink." I wanted everything to be just right. I was pacing back and forth in a frenzy, moving things around and pondering how I would ask. I hadn't even taken my coat off.

After about ten minutes of asking me if I was okay, Trina became very suspicious. I quickly fled the scene, ducking into the bathroom so that she wouldn't be able to see right through me. I could hear her footsteps coming toward the bathroom. I froze; I didn't know what to do. I grabbed the first thing I saw, a toothbrush, and began brushing my teeth. She appeared at the door and looked at me as I stood there, with toothpaste all over my mouth, brushing frantically in my suit and overcoat. "What the heck is the matter with you?" I calmly replied, "Nothing, why do you ask?" She shook her head and said, "I don't know what's going on, but you'd better tell me soon," as she went and sat back down.

I looked in the mirror and thought, *Okay, Craig, it's now or never. Don't think; just do it.* Trying desperately to build up my courage, I went to the bedroom and got a tape of Trina's favorite song. I put it in the stereo in the kitchen and cued it up without her noticing. Then I went to the living room and shut off the television. Trina looked up at me with venomous eyes, which indicated I was about to get the blast of a lifetime. Still with my coat on, I said, "Before you say anything, please just listen. There is a reason why I am acting so crazy. It's because of you. I have been thinking about us all day. About everything we have been through and everything we have been fighting about. I made some decisions."

I walked over to the stereo and pressed 'play,' then gently reached for Trina's hand. With the music in the background, I asked for a dance. Shocked, she asked, "What are you doing?" as we started to dance. I backed away to sing along with the song, "I Cross My Heart" by George Strait. After the words faded away, I knelt down on one knee and looked up at Trina. I pulled the ring from my pocket, took a very deep breath, and in a gentle voice asked, "Will you marry me?" A small smile appeared on her face as she paused for a moment and then whispered, "Yes."

We embraced and shared a kiss, looking into each other's eyes and saying, "I love you." I did it! I actually did it! All of a sudden, as we stood there staring at each other, there was a loud knock at the door. Trina looked at me, puzzled, and I was a bit surprised at the moment as well. I went and opened the door, and it was the limousine driver!

He congratulated both of us and looked at Trina, motioning for her to come outside. His exact words were, "Your carriage awaits." What timing! It was perfect. He looked over at me and I nodded in appreciation as he smiled back, knowing he was in for a big tip. Quietly to myself, I whispered, "Well, Amen!" I wrapped Trina's coat around her, quickly grabbed the bottle of champagne and roses to surprise her with, and headed out the door.

The look on Trina's face when she saw the limousine was priceless! She was in awe. As we sat in the back together, we looked over at each other, and I knew in that moment that I was in control of my life. We took off into the night as soulmates, engaged to be married. It was the most incredible feeling. It felt good, really good.

That was a day I will never forget. The rest of the evening was exciting and incredibly eventful as we picked up the rest of the family. They all thought I had won the lottery and were surprised and perhaps a little disappointed when they learned I hadn't, but we had a great night of celebration and they were all very happy for Trina and me.

That was the first time I made the decision to let go of the pain I was carrying around and the anger I had about my parents' divorce. By forgiving myself and listening to my heart, I found my spirit and was able to let go.

After Trina and I were married and we were on our honeymoon, she asked how I had known that she was "the one." I thought about it for a bit, then rattled off some of the obvious reasons I knew I should give, about how loving, caring, honest, smart, and beautiful she was. Then I looked at her and said, "You know, I just knew. I felt it. No matter how much I thought about it, I could not imagine my life without you in it. It was your spirit. You taught me I could trust and love and that we could build a life together if I would just let go and own my own life."

Acceptance or Closure

Children of divorce are unwittingly presented with an explosive beginning to a lifelong healing journey. It's a traumatic event that impacts the rest of our lives. It can continue to haunt our souls with lingering anger and pain, greatly affecting our choices as we continue to encounter new life experiences and move into new phases of our lives, like marriage. Sometimes it seems we will never find a complete ending. There will always be something new sneaking up or old issues being brought up again and again. Therefore, I don't believe that achieving closure regarding my parents' divorce is possible for me.

Does divorce ever end? I don't think it does. It becomes part of you, part of your family, and part of your life. For example, situations such as the following might arise:

- Attend a family wedding and you could find yourself caught in a family feud where you end up playing the referee.
- One of your parents might bring a new date that you don't really like to Thanksgiving dinner.

- Your mom or dad might ask you probing questions about how the other is doing, and you find yourself caught stuck for words because you're scared to hurt anyone.
- New stepbrothers and stepsisters could come to you with their problems, compounding your own.
- As you're planning your child's birthday party, you might find you need two different dates, or you live in fear and pray that your parents will be civil to each other.
- Your friend's parents divorce and it reminds you of what you went through and the pain you still carry.
- After deciding to get married, you experience tremendous fear that divorce could happen to you.
- People you love question your parents' behavior and you find yourself overwhelmed with anger.

There are so many things that sneak up to remind us and sometimes even add more to our bottled-up hurt.

It has been thirteen years since my parents split up, but I can guarantee that one of these days, the phone will ring and there will be some new divorce-related issue for me to deal with. It's a scary thought to me, thinking it will never end—but it's true.

Acceptance is the answer. It becomes a journey where we need to take one step at a time—learning, hurting, feeling, and working through it issue by issue. We must accept the situation in order to find some peace and heal.

We can bring closure to certain feelings, situations, issues, or problems that we faced during the divorce journey. We can work through each one and come to a positive conclusion by deciding to accept it or let it go and move on. However, trying to find closure and bury the whole divorce experience so that we will never have to deal with it again—that just doesn't happen.

So what do we do? Accept it. Accept it as a part of who we are and know it is not what we are. We have the ability to create our own future the way we want it to be. We may have more things to deal with—more pain to come, more obstacles to conquer, and more victories to win. That's life! However, each of these situations causes us to grow stronger and gain the courage, wisdom, confidence, and strength to deal with new events or resurfacing issues that we are faced with. With acceptance comes the ability to let go and control our own lives, problems, and circumstances. That is something we simply couldn't have as children journeying through a divorce.

The divorce will be with me wherever I go and whatever I do. I know deep down that because I have come this far in my healing journey, I will be ready to deal with each new circumstance, each new curveball. This will make me stronger, smarter, healthier, and more of a person than I am today.

Communication is the Key

To let go of the pain and the hurt, it is essential for children of divorce to talk about their true feelings with their parents. Divorce is a breeding ground for a lack of communication. After my parents divorced, there were many times that I felt I shouldn't talk to them about how I felt. It seemed like somehow I had become an inconvenience, and I didn't want to bother them seeing as they were in such a crisis. Other times, I was so scared and upset about how I felt that I could barely allow myself to feel the feelings, let alone talk about them. What if what I was thinking about was true? I wanted to spare myself the pain. I spent a long time hating myself for one big reason: I didn't know if my parents loved me, and I couldn't ask.

Because I didn't discuss things with my parents, I made bad choices, choices I regret to this day—such as giving up my hockey dream. However, eventually I did choose to talk to Mom and Dad. At first, it was only when I couldn't take any more and my feelings had built up to a boiling point. At these times I no longer cared who I hurt, so I let them have it. It was not the most productive way to talk about my feelings, but over time I learned a big lesson—that no matter what, parents love their children. My parents loved me, and because they told me they did and that it was okay for me to love both of them, we grew closer. That opened the door for communication.

We need to ask the hard questions as well as the stupid or ridiculous questions. We need to confront our fears and take time to talk to ourselves. We need to feel supported and we need to feel loved. To fill these needs, and to help us understand, we have to talk and ask questions. Unfortunately, we don't always get an answer. However, it helps to get problems off our chest and to a place where we can begin to work on them. As children of divorce, we should not be afraid of how we feel. It's not wrong or right; it's simply how we feel. Communication and patience are crucial keys to letting go and moving on with our own lives.

What is the Answer to Letting Go?

Many people ask the question, "How do you let go of the pain? How do you forget and move on?" I don't know if there is just one answer, but I know what worked for me. I decided to accept and forgive—forgive my parents and myself.

We can choose to understand better by looking at things in a new way in order to make peace and forgive. Eventually, the goal is to move on with our own lives and families in a loving way. I don't believe we can ever forget, but we can forgive. I know I will never forget the hurt I felt after the divorce. However, searching for the truth and accepting that we may never understand the reasons why; realizing we are all human and make mistakes; and ultimately, learning to love ourselves and find our true spirit—all of these things give us the courage to confront our ghosts and forgive.

I have been able to forgive my parents for divorcing because I can now forgive myself for my own mistakes and my anger. I believe learning to let go is ultimately the beginning to truly finding our spirit and healing after divorce.

CHAPTER TEN

Healing and Finding Wisdom

"Eavesdrop on your heart and be courageous enough to accept and trust what it reveals. It is your beacon of light through the fog of insecurity."

~Keith Sanheim

Time heals your wounds ... your pain ... your soul ... your heart ... and your spirit. Great wisdom comes from great lessons of the heart. Time, courage, and wisdom are what I believe we, as survivors of a family crisis, must use to heal our broken hearts and embrace our lives! As we continue to go through life, we are sure to come across more challenges, uncontrollable circumstances, and all kinds of issues we need to deal with. Some of these circumstances may be extremely painful, like divorce—and some of them might be the most exciting times of our lives! What we choose to do with these situations will greatly shape the rest of our lives.

The truth is, no matter how great the pain or how hard the situation, we are faced with choice in every problem we encounter. I believe the secret, if there is one, boils down to one bottom line—simply put, our attitude and perception. Because we know in our hearts that we can find opportunities and better our lives, we need only choose to do so. Keep an open mind and an open heart, and give it time. At the same time, know that it is just never that easy. We have to work at it. I would agree with you if you were to say to me that it is hard to find opportunities in extremely painful situations.

Hard, yes—but not impossible. Faith will bring us what we need during the tragedies we face.

Positive solutions to difficult times linger in our minds with the same vitality as do negative solutions. I believe our attitude and courage help define what our life choices will be. Whether we let the pain of divorce control us or take control by confronting our issues and loving ourselves is for only us to decide. As we walk the journey through divorce, we learn and grow every day from both good and bad circumstances. This is ultimately what helps build our character and increase our wisdom.

Albert Einstein once said that a human being can possess only one of two states of mind at any given time: faith or fear. It seems so simple when you think about it. Despite the insane mess of emotions and confusion, in the end our attitude and perception boil down to one ultimate choice: Faith or Fear!

Happiness Is What I Want

Finding happiness after my parents' divorce seemed as likely as the Pope getting married. No chance of it! Many years passed where I felt like I would never be happy again. It took me a long time to realize that what I was really searching for wasn't just the feeling of being happy, but also the ability to like myself and be happy about who I was.

Late one night, back when I was working at the restaurant, I came to a realization about happiness. I learned that happiness is really just an emotion in need of a positive and empowering state of mind. I was mopping up the kitchen floor at the time, getting ready to close. I remember the night distinctly, because I was very depressed about my life at the time. I was filled with a tremendous amount of self-doubt, constantly questioning my family issues and my future. However, I was slowly starting to make a small but positive emotional climb back from the depths of rock bottom. On this particular night, I discovered for myself a door to the pathway of true happiness.

It feels like it was yesterday, as I remember so clearly asking myself, *Why can't I just be happy?* As I wrung out the wet, grease-covered mop over the sink, I thought, *Why can't I wake up one day and feel good about my life, happy about who I am? Why does everything seem to go wrong? Am I cursed or something?* I didn't want to feel depressed and lost anymore. I didn't want to be alone anymore. I didn't want to feel like I hated everything. I wanted to bring the joy back into my life—the happy times I had been longing for.

At the time, I had come to this great conclusion about life, finally understanding that life is what you make it—but no matter how hard I tried, I couldn't seem to feel happy. I didn't know how. It seemed like I had to be on guard all the time, fearing what would happen to me next. I felt like the next crisis was just lurking around the corner. I found myself working so hard in all directions, trying with such great effort to get my life on track—and yet I never allowed myself to be happy about it. I wished happiness could somehow just fall from the sky and land in my lap.

I was putting the mop away and preparing to go home for the night when my boss peeked in from the dining room and said, "Craig, come here a minute." I knew that tone, and I wondered what he could possibly want me to do now. It was almost midnight and it had been a really long day. I had written three exams at school that day and then delivered pizza all night. I still needed to study for my last final exam, which was the next morning. I just wanted to go home.

Of course, my boss had another idea. He could be very eccentric and quite the dictator when he wanted to be, but I could never have imagined what he had in store for me. I walked through my neatly mopped kitchen and into the dining room to see what he wanted. He was sitting on a barstool, sipping a drink of hot coffee. "Craig," he said, "We had a customer in tonight who commented on how dusty and filthy the ceiling tiles and ceiling fans are." I nodded my head in agreement and suggested, "Yes, they could probably use a cleaning," thinking he meant in a month or so, and figuring it would be done by a cleaning company. My boss said, "Good. Get to work."

In amazement, I stammered, "Right now? The whole dining room ceiling ... you need equipment for that." He shook his head and said, "Craig, it has to be done. There is a vacuum in the back; use that. We're paying you, aren't we?" In defeat, I said, "Yeah, but ... but ... oh man," and dragged my butt to the back room. I really, really didn't want to do this, and I said to myself, "Vacuum the ceiling? This is crazy!"

I found the vacuum and a ladder in the back storage room, but the vacuum didn't have a vacuum head to go with it—just the little hose attachment. There was no way I was going to vacuum the whole dining room ceiling with the little hose attachment! It would take hours! I went to my boss to protest and he looked at me as though he wasn't listening to a thing I said. "Do it anyway. Just get the bad spots. Do a good job and you can grab yourself a beer or two." I looked at him with a mortified expression on my face, trying to indicate that this was nuts. I thought, *Oh yippee, I get a beer. How about going home?* But he kept sipping his coffee and put his head down to read the paper. Absolutely frustrated, I went back to the storage room to gather the useless vacuum, the ladder, and a rag. Then, unwillingly, I went to work—debating whether or not I should just quit.

I positioned the ladder in front of the bay window in order to work my way back towards the kitchen, then began vacuuming with the tiny hose. An hour and a half went by extremely slowly, and I had barely made a dent. I hadn't even cleaned half of the ceiling, and it didn't look like it was making much of a difference. I couldn't believe I was actually doing this. It had to be the stupidest thing I have ever done, and I was just steaming inside. It's amazing how many things run through a person's mind in that type of a position and mood.

It led me to thinking about my desire to be happy. My mind was racing like crazy, ideas and thoughts zooming in and out. I can't explain it, but for whatever reason, a poem flashed into my mind. Maybe it was the late hour, my lack of sleep, or the burst of energy that came from my anger—but regardless, I was inspired. I jumped off the ladder and grabbed a napkin to write down all the things I was thinking. This poem is what came out:

Happiness

Does it come from the mind?
Does it come from the heart…

Is it something one receives?
Or is it something one perceives…

Is it created through riches?
Is it created through thought?
Is it something that is learned?
Or something that is taught…

I wonder if it is really a thing
or a feeling we get
That only life can bring.

I found my answer when I looked inside,
And felt my heart open wide…

I felt what happiness is all about,
For your true inner beauty is what brings
happiness out…

My boss came over to check on me. He was obviously getting tired too, and asked, "Craig, how much longer will you be?" Barely finished half, but eagerly wanting to go home, I said, "Oh, I will be done in two minutes!" He said, "Good, I will go lock up and we can get out of here." I don't think he ever knew the difference.

It felt like a door opened for me when I wrote my poem. I realized that happiness was about me, not my circumstances. Life is what you make it, and I had to create my life and decide who I really was and what I wanted to become. I had to feel good about my life in order to make it happy. I needed to look inside my heart and ask myself where I had been in order to know where I wanted to go! I had never stopped to think about my past or congratulate myself on how far I had come, to determine what I had learned and how I could better my future. Instead, I had been wrapped up in desperately trying to find something in the present that would fill my void and make me happy. I had been unwilling to actually work towards what I truly wanted.

Life is truly a gift and happiness is an emotion we feel based on our life's choices. In order to find the happiness that our spirits seek, we need to create our own priorities and develop balance in our lives. Sometimes we will need to do what is right despite how awkward or difficult it may be, instead of what will make us happy at the present moment, by focusing on our long-term vision. Sometimes, the universe seems to show us our true beauty in our most difficult times when we least expect it.

Finding Your Heart's Purpose

Have a dream. Find your passion and live your dream, whatever it may be! Have you ever asked yourself what your life is all about? Not the everyday stuff or the daily routine, but what's inside you, where passions bloom within your soul! Have you ever thought about your life's purpose? What you really want to do in your life?

I came to a conclusion about life when I asked myself those very questions. I believe with all my heart that we are here to contribute our own unique gifts to the world. We need only identify what those gifts are and create a purpose behind them—a "heart's purpose."

The greatest lesson my parents' divorce taught me was to have a heart's purpose. I learned this through my journey of self-love. Even as I write this sentence, I am still today working on my journey of self-love and on my self-esteem. After years of striving to keep a positive attitude, there are still many times when I find myself doubting my abilities, my limitations, what I can achieve, and what I can really become. Being human, it is easy to fall into being focused on the fear side of the spectrum. When others criticize, attempts fail, the world seems like it's crashing down, or you feel you've lost your purpose or your dream, it's so easy to give up.

Create passion in your life from the things you feel strong desire for, the things that create fire in your belly and allow you to access the little spark of courage that picks you up and keeps you going. No matter what, never quit! Own your mistakes and failures, as they will teach you lessons you can grow from and lead you in the direction you need to go. At the same time, make sure to congratulate and appreciate yourself for the successes along the way, no matter how little they may be.

My mom once told me a story about a person's value. She had read it over the internet from an email she had received. It really opened my eyes and got under my skin, and it has become embedded in my mind for life. She said: "A speaker entered the room, waving a clean, crisp hundred-dollar bill as he walked up to the podium. He held the money high above his head and said, 'Who here tonight would like to have this clean, crisp, good-looking hundred-dollar bill?' All of those in attendance raised their hands in acceptance. The gentleman then crunched and crumpled up the hundred-dollar bill in his hand. He again lifted it high above his head, looked to the crowd and said, 'Who here tonight would like to have this crushed and crinkled hundred-dollar bill?' They all raised their hands. He then took the hundred-dollar bill, tossed it on the floor, and began stepping and jumping on it. He picked it up, smashed it in his hands again, and then stepped on it one more time, making sure it was good and dirty. Then he picked it up, held it high above his head, and asked the crowd, 'Who here tonight would like this torn, stepped on, beaten up, dirty, tattered hundred-dollar bill?' Again, all hands went up. The audience knew that even though the hundred-dollar bill had nearly been destroyed, it was still worth one hundred dollars. The gentleman laid the decrepit bill on the table and said, 'Like this hundred-dollar bill, you can be stepped on, torn apart, beaten up, and dumped on—but you will never lose your value!'"

You never lose your value. Regardless of the problems divorce brings or the life choices you make, and however long it takes you to get to where you want to go, you are as valuable at this moment as you will be in your finest hour. For a long time, I didn't get it. I always saw myself as nothing, without the things I wanted or wanted to be, rather than seeing myself as already being what I want and moving towards my goals one step at a time. I learned that what you believe you are, you will become.

Let me ask you a question: Do you remember the last time you completely lost track of time in something you were doing? Think back; close your eyes. What was that something? Really think about it. My guess is that you will find your little gifts and your passions in those times of your life. Imagine the hidden talents you may find lurking inside, waiting to be released into the world if you choose to acknowledge them.

Finding your heart's purpose is a mixture of identifying your talents and passions, finding a worthwhile cause, believing in yourself, and ultimately having a dream! I believe that creating a heart's purpose is an unending task. It's not like a goal you work towards completing one day. It is something you strive to do and be. It gives you reason to carry out your goals. Mother Theresa was a woman true to her purpose, and because of it, she accomplished great achievements in her life. Her purpose was unending and felt around the world, even after she died. She was a genuine hero.

Ask yourself right now what your unique talents are. What is it that you love to do? Who are some of your heroes and mentors and why? What is it that you're striving for? What's your vision? Where do you need to start? What things can you do to carry out your heart's purpose? What makes you special? Take time to think about these questions. Sometimes you will find that the answers come immediately; other times, it will take longer.

When I started answering my questions and listening to my desires, I let go of all the reasons I had given myself for why I couldn't do something, be something, and have something. I finally heard what my heart was saying. I heard that I truly wanted more from my life. I heard that I had some talent that I wanted to contribute to the world, despite the hardships I have gone through in my life. I heard that I had a dream!

In the game of life, like many other children, I got dealt the divorce hand. Sometimes I had to fold my cards and other times I had to ask for another card when I needed it. As I continued to play, I realized that if I wanted to live my dream, I had to bust through my fears and risk changing my pair for five of a kind! Win, lose, or draw!

Sometimes, the events in our lives—especially the ones that impact us at such an enormous level, like divorce—act as clues that can bring us closer to our dreams. My dream became about making a difference in my life so that I could make a positive difference in other people's lives, inspiring them to live their dreams.

I would like to share my heart's purpose with you, and I encourage you to write yours. My Heart's Purpose is: *Through my commitment to excellence and personal achievement, everything I do and all the actions I take in my life are for the purpose of teaching, motivating, and inspiring all individuals who desire to achieve more in their lives and live their dreams.*

What is your dream? Why not stop and ask yourself? Determine whether you are truly living the life you want to be. If you are, I congratulate you! But if you're not, why not take some action towards a life that you do want, as hard as that may be? If anything, the divorce taught me that life is truly too short and it is not meant for us to watch it go by. Own it, love it, engulf its essence, and live it to the fullest.

We all have to face adversity in life, confront our fears, and struggle to survive. Why not face your dreams, too? If we can overcome so much, I believe we can also accomplish everything we desire in our hearts.

To find your heart's purpose
You must look beyond, beyond the surface

Deep into the pith of your life
Slash through all your fears and doubts with a mental knife.

Look farther, past reason, past your goal
And touch your spirit to awaken your soul!

Moving On With My Own Family

I sat peacefully in a dimly lit hospital room, rocking back and forth with my newly born daughter, Briana Ashley, cradled in my arms. It was shortly after 2:30 AM and I was in awe of the miracle that had just happened and the realization that I was actually living one of my dreams. Exhausted, Trina had fallen asleep, so I got night duty. Filled with bliss, I examined Briana's beautiful wrinkled baby skin and her delicate tiny fingers and toes. I watched her little eyes flicker, trying to stay open as she too fell asleep. I felt overwhelmed with joy and wonder, and many questions entered my mind as I contemplated the future now that my name had changed to Daddy.

I asked myself, "What will I teach Briana? What will she want to do in her life? What will her favorite foods or color be? Will she like to sing and dance, play sports, or travel the world? Will she be more like Trina or me? Whose bad habits will she get?" I couldn't believe I was actually holding my baby daughter. I started to reminisce about how I had been pulling my hair out in anticipation of her birth, scared of my new responsibilities.

I remember being a complete wreck, wanting to guarantee that I would be a good father and husband and provide a good family home for my children. As I moved on to the next journey with my own family, I thought about how I wanted to give my children more—a better life than I had and more opportunity. I think that as parents, we all want that. I still fight my fear of making the same mistakes that my parents did, because divorce is something I never want my children to have to endure.

I have realized that Briana and my other children will be affected by my parents' divorce. As they grow up, they will have questions about why Grandma and Grandpa don't live together and why they don't love each other anymore. They will look to me for understanding, guidance, and answers about what family means. This creates a new fear in me about how to address their questions, and it challenges me to decide what it is that I really want to teach them.

I also know that some of my fears and unresolved issues will affect my relationship with my children. After Briana was born, I realized the only way I could create a quality relationship with her would be to give her me, and not my fears. For that reason, it has become important for me to face my shadows and ghosts. I believe I need to heal my wounds in order to be able to teach my children the lessons I want them to learn. I can give more of myself and be a better example for them. I truly believe we need to make an effort to heal our past wounds and let go in order to move on and not carry those issues into our own families.

As I watched Briana sleep that very first night, childhood memories flashed through my mind. I remembered the good things about growing up—hockey, family trips, watching movies, having fun— and how, despite the divorce, my parents did a great job raising my brother and me. I wanted that for my daughter. I promised her I would provide a great family life and lots of love, always. I promised her I would always be there when she needed me. She lay there, so precious and so fragile, yet I could see in her little eyes that she had a strong soul. I realized in that moment, as I moved into my new journey of fatherhood, that the greatest gift I could give would be my unconditional love.

Definition of Family

Throughout my journey, I spent many long hours analyzing what my family had become now that we were no longer the "Leibel Family." I contemplated many options, trying to define and unlock the true meaning of the word *family*. At the beginning of my parents' separation, I was desperate to hold onto my family unit and have something that made me feel like I belonged. The traditional family I had pictured—two parents and children, all living in the same house with a white picket fence—was tossed out the window when my parents divorced.

Along the way, I realized I had to mourn and grieve my loss in order to let go of the family I had grown up with and loved. However, at the same time, I still needed to feel that I was connected and a part of something meaningful and important. I knew I needed to redefine my divided family, but I didn't know how.

The Collins dictionary describes family as: "a group of parents and their children, one's spouse and children and a group descended from a common ancestor." Reading the dictionary definition over and over in my head, I began contemplating. What really makes up a family?

All kinds of ideas started to bloom in my head as I pondered that question, but it wasn't until I started writing down my ideas that it finally hit me. It took me a long time to find my answer, but I did. As I wrote down what my family meant to me, rather than looking at it strictly as a set structure or hierarchy, I found that my definition expanded and I let go of my ideals. I began plotting some ideas about what family and family members mean to me:

- Someone to go to when you're feeling upset or have a problem.
- People who support you and teach you right from wrong.
- People to share experiences and lessons with as you win and lose in the game of life.
- The security of knowing people who love you just because you are you.
- People to spend time with, doing activities for fun or "just because."
- Loved ones you can turn to for help when you're in trouble.
- People who will stand by your side in both bad and good times.
- People who cheer you on when you reach for the sky.

- People to help you with important decisions in your life.
- People who will always love you, no matter what you do.
- An environment in which to grow together and set building blocks for the foundation of your life.
- Enjoying the fun roles we play in our family (i.e., oldest child, middle child, or baby of the family). These roles work to give us purpose and responsibilities in our families.

The more I thought, the more I wrote and the broader my definition of family became. I kept writing for almost an hour, but I still couldn't pinpoint it or define my connection in one single sentence. One thing I could really grab onto was that family means so many different things.

As I began rereading everything I had written, I felt it still seemed to need some structure. I needed a description to define how families are united—mother, father, son, daughter, grandparents, uncles, aunts, and so on.

Then, like a sudden burst of energy, I found my answer hidden behind all of my sentences. There was one underlying truth in everything I thought and felt my family was. I had unlocked my puzzle, redefining my divided family and identifying my belief. I had come up with my own definition, and the best part was that it was only one sentence. It felt so incredible, so real, to know in my heart that my answer was what was true for me. I now knew deep inside that I belonged. I knew my place.

I thank you for spending this time with me and would like to leave you with one last thought. My definition of family, and what I believe is the true meaning of the word:

People united by the bond of unconditional love!

Conclusion

Dear Friend,

I would like to share a personal note with you if I may. *To read is to explore other's thoughts; to write is to capture your own!* Writing *Within a Child's Heart* has been the most profound healing journey I have ever experienced—a journey of exploration of my heart, my life, and myself. I needed to express many painful moments and ask myself honestly how I felt about them in order to process the emotions, identify the truth, and make my conclusions. By learning to accept and own my feelings, I discovered many pearls of wisdom that life's lessons give us from time to time.

Writing became a powerful tool for me. It brought to paper what lies within my heart. It helped me release my deepest pains, hurts, and sorrows, and to face some fears in order to triumph over them. I found confidence by taking control of my life, and it helped me to love me for who I am and what I want to be. As well, I was able to resolve some issues I had been hanging onto for years, and open up a healing door for my family members.

Writing can be an empowering tool for anyone dealing with a divorce or other life issues. It can be private or shared with whomever you choose. Take out a piece of paper when you're feeling like you have something to say or when you are confused about things in your life. Journal your thoughts, your feelings, and your discoveries.

You may discover the lessons you are supposed to learn, or you may simply feel better. When we get hurt in life, it leaves an open wound. If we touch our wound, it hurts, and if we don't take care of it properly, it will get worse and leave a scar. However, when we do take care of it, over time it will heal. Through my writing, I have come to realize that we have to want to take action to heal the cuts and repair the scars of our parents' divorce. We can then start to take control of our lives, overcome adversity, rise above our circumstances, and stand triumphant and victorious!

I encourage everyone to write in order to help heal your wounds. Through your courage to face your fears, you will find the wisdom you seek and grow into the potential that you know deep down you have.

Enjoy writing.

"Although it was a hard road to travel, my parents' divorce caused me to be like mortar in the hands of a mason. It molded me into the strong-willed person I am today. I was left empty and with a feeling of abandonment, and I spent a lifetime mistrusting others, demanding independence, and seeking stability. I resented responsibility as I felt forced into an adult world to raise my sibilings. However, as I entered adulthood I realized that the responsibility, mistakes, and vulnerability I experienced during the turmoil taught me to empathize with myself, communicate my problems, and avoid sabotaging my own relationships with fear and pain. It allowed me to control my future."

~Michelle Keylor

www.withinachildsheart.com

The Foundation for Families in Transformation (FFIT) offers a free-of-charge program called RAINBOWS, which provides children and their families with an opportunity to deal with grief and loss. RAINBOWS offers a support-group curriculum for children who have suffered significant loss in their lives—through death, divorce, or other painful transitions. There are separate programs designed for young children and adolescents.

RAINBOWS provides these children with an opportunity to meet new friends who have shared similar experiences; to have trained, caring adults present while they sort through and understand their grief; and to achieve a healthy acceptance of what has happened to their families.

The aim of RAINBOWS is to implant in these grieving children a belief in their own goodness and in the value of their families. The curriculum teaches that each change in life is an occasion for a new beginning. The goal of the support group is to assist children in expressing and understanding their feelings, accepting what has happened, and experiencing a sense of belonging and love.

It doesn't need to hurt forever.

Please accept this invitation to help support RAINBOWS.
GIVING 101: You Can Make a DIFFERENCE in a CHILD'S LIFE!

Divorce Hurts—RAINBOWS Helps

Name:_____

Address:_____

City:_____ Province/State:_____

Postal/Zip code:_____

Please mail cheques to FFIT/RAINBOWS, 10530-110 Street, Edmonton, AB T5H 3C5

For more information, call: (780) 448-1180 or 1-800-416-4673